And No One Saw It Coming

MARCI GLIDDEN SAVAGE

ISBN 978-1-66780-058-5
eBook ISBN 978-1-66780-059-2

Dedicated to my children
Kris, Cory, and Dani,

Amid a very difficult and tragic loss, your strength to move forward, your courage to be vulnerable, your tenacity to grapple and reconcile with the truth, and your willingness to forgive - are nothing short of inspiring.

You are my greatest joy!
Love you more!
Mom

In Loving Memory of
Paul Burnett Glidden
(August 20, 1955 – August 13, 2014)

And

Michael Alan Savage
(February 26, 1961 – March 15, 2019)

CONTENTS

FORWARD

"Owning our story can be hard but not nearly as difficult as spending our lives running from it. Embracing our vulnerabilities is risky but not nearly as dangerous as giving up on love and belonging and joy—the experiences that make us the most vulnerable. Only when we are brave enough to explore the darkness will we discover the infinite power of our light."[1]
–Brené Brown, PhD, LMSW

CHAPTER 1

Open Letter to Mental Illness

"At the root of this dilemma is the way we view mental health in this country. Whether an illness affects your heart, your leg or your brain, it's still an illness, and there should be no distinction." [1]

—Michelle Obama

TO: MENTAL ILLNESS

You are a formidable and treasonous opponent. You hide in plain sight because you are a master at disguises. That's your Ace in the hole—your secret weapon of war.

Shhh, don't tell. Your power depends on silence.

You are politically correct, and you don't discriminate. You're not gender-specific. You're not racist. You don't lean left or right; you are independent. Age is not relevant to you; anyone at any age will do. You don't care about social or economic status or religious affiliation. You're an equal opportunity disease.

Shhh, don't tell. Your power depends on silence.

You quietly hide behind the usual and customary outward behaviors. You cohabitate simultaneously with laughter, love, success, compassion, faith, commitment, trust, sincerity, honesty, and intelligence. Thus, making your identity that much harder to see.

Shhh, don't tell. Your power depends on silence.

Your bag of tricks is endless. You amassed a multiple-symptom arsenal, so vast and so varied that most of your symptoms can be associated with other diseases. Like cancer, heart disease, ALS, Alzheimer's, AIDS, diabetes, and the like, your peers also have multiple symptoms and can be undiagnosed or misdiagnosed. And sometimes death precedes a diagnosis, just like you.

Shhh, don't tell. Your power depends on silence.

You are content to watch our efforts to eradicate and eliminate your peers silently. Funds easily raised, and research applauded for "real" diseases. Pharmaceutical companies are encouraged to produce new and experimental drugs and provide clinical trials for even the slightest chance of a cure. Treatment centers built. Slogans adapted with words like Hope and Cure and Fight. Runners garner donations for 5K and 10Ks, while crowds march. Celebrities host telethons, and musicians produce world concerts. Contributions garnered for "real diseases," and T-shirts are worn. And those in the battle with these opponents are brave-courageous-survivors, as they should be!

Shhh, don't tell. Your power depends on silence.

You willingly attach your name to words like crazy, deranged, insane, lunatic, and madness. Your knowledge of how cultures, societies, and the world views unusual, different, odd, or "crazy" behavior in people has given you an edge. In your game of deception, you want the world to only recognize you in "those" behaviors…in "those people"…in "those" actions.

Shhh, don't tell. Your power depends on silence.

Day after day and night after night, you convince your victim that they must keep you a secret. You whisper, "No one will understand." "They will think you are crazy or weak." "You need to nut-up."

Shhh, don't tell. Your power depends on silence.

You disrupt sleep patterns, and you silence communication. You isolate, produce anxiety, and distort the truth. You applaud depression. You celebrate chronic worry, feelings of fear, and the "coup de grace"—hopelessness.

Shhh, don't tell. Your power depends on silence.

You change your modus operandi often to stay at the top of your game. Patiently you lie in wait, hiding in the shadows and stealthily flying under the radar. You emphasize perceived failures. You systematically slam shut every door of hope. You ebb and flow over days, weeks, months, and years.

Shhh, don't tell. Your power depends on silence.

And when all your lies, deceitfulness, trickery, and deviousness have obliterated any hope, you release your final weapon—PAIN. Pain so severe and powerful that only agony, torment, and despair remain. Pain so intense that the love of family, friends, and life itself can't be felt or seen. Just the pain. Only Pain. And with your final assassin's whisper, "There is only one way to end the pain"…they're gone. Forever.

Game over and game on.

I will tell.

I won't stop.

You can count on it.

CHAPTER 2

Before the Tempest

"The heart of a man is very much like the sea; it has its storms, it has its tides, and in its depths, it has its pearls too." [1]
—**Vincent van Gogh,** *The Letters of Vincent van Gogh*

I could hear his jacked-up, blue '65 Mustang with headers and deep-dish Cragar wheels coming from blocks away. He was so hot! But he had a girlfriend, my friend Colleen who lived across the street. Colleen and her twin sister, Corinne, were high school seniors, and I was a sophomore. It was the fall of 1972, and I had recently moved to California from Texas. My dad's company transferred him to Southern California as a Western Region Sales Manager. Although my dad's office was on Wilshire Blvd. in downtown Los Angeles, my parents bought a house eighty miles south in Fountain Valley, a city located in Orange County. Fountain Valley is a neighboring town to the more famous Huntington Beach, known as "Surf

City, USA." In 1972, there was a significant influx of residents into the area. The high school I attended had the largest student population west of the Mississippi River, with 4,500 students.

I was born in Texas and lived there most of my childhood, except for one year. In 1969, my dad received a promotion, and we moved to Memphis, Tennessee. I was so excited when we moved back to Texas the following year when I was thirteen. Texas was home to me, and I thought I would always live in Texas like generations of ancestors before me. The summer before my sophomore year in high school, my parents announced that we were moving once again to Southern California. I was devastated. I had just made the high school drill team! And in a big football-loving state like Texas, making the drill team was second to a cheerleading squad. In Texas in the seventies, junior high school was seventh through ninth grade, and high school was tenth through twelfth. But in California, high school was ninth through twelfth grade. Not only would I be moving and going to a new school, but I would also be entering the new high school as a sophomore when all the other students entered as freshmen.

Even worse, I was moving away from my best friend, Jaci. Jaci and I were inseparable; if we weren't in school or sleeping, Jaci and I were together. Like many fourteen-year-old girls in the early seventies, we spent hours talking about secret crushes on boys, decorating our bedrooms with blacklight posters and peace signs, and listening to Carol King's *Tapestry* album or Don McLean's iconic song, "American Pie." We enjoyed riding our matching 10-speed bikes to the local 7-Eleven store for a Slurpee or shopping for a new pair of bellbottom jeans or hot pants. How could my parents move me away from my best friend and to California of all places? I cried for weeks, hoping my parents would change their minds, but to no avail.

This 5'8" blue-eyed girl with long brown hair and a BIG Texas accent arrived on a Friday in Southern California in September 1972. I spent the weekend worrying about starting a new school the following Monday. I couldn't believe how different Fountain Valley High School was from the schools I attended in Texas. I came from a very conservative junior high school with a stringent dress code: knee-length skirts, no sleeveless shirts, no jeans, and the boys couldn't have sideburns or long hair. As I walked around the laid-back, coastal community high school campus, I couldn't believe students were chewing gum in class, wearing shorts, t-shirts, and flip-flops. And everyone talked with an accent! (It took me a while to figure out that it was me who had the accent.)

Eventually, I found my way and made new friends. Settling into the California lifestyle was a smoother transition than I expected, probably because Huntington Beach was a short ten-minute drive away. What teenager wouldn't like hanging out at the beach every day during the summer, watching those cute surfers with their sun-kissed long hair, tans, and easy-going, hang loose attitudes? Oh, and that boy I mentioned earlier, the one who drove that loud, blue Mustang? He happened to be one of those cute surfers. His name was Paul Glidden. Sometimes after school or on the weekends, I would hang out with Paul and the twins across the street. Paul was easy to talk to and always fun to be around. He was adorable, and I secretly wished he wasn't Colleen's boyfriend.

After Paul and Colleen broke up, Paul and I remained friends and kept in contact. Over the next year, we continued to talk on the phone. Occasionally, we ran into each other at the beach. We enjoyed each other's company and the flirtatious nature of our conversations, even though we both were dating other people. Paul called me one evening in March 1975, and after several minutes of our usual small talk and catching up, Paul finally asked me out on a date. What? Finally, Paul Glidden, the cute, hot surfer boy I had a secret crush on, was asking me out on a date! Bad news—I had a boyfriend, Steve, a freshman at the University of California, San Diego, and we had been dating for almost a year. I couldn't believe I had to say no. Uggggh!

I sensed Paul's disappointment over the phone, and I think he could feel mine, too. Paul and his friend, Tab, crewed on Tab's father's 35' Erickson sailboat out of Long Beach every Wednesday. Paul wanted to take me sailing on a double date with his friend, Tab, and his girlfriend, Terri. I had never been sailing, much less with a boy I secretly liked. I felt terrible! After I hung up the phone, I called my best friend. I remember so well the phone conversation and advice.

She said, "Marci, you have liked Paul for such a long time. I know you're dating Steve, but I know you like Paul a lot. Right?"

And because you tell your best friend forever (BFF) in high school EVERYTHING, I said, "Yes, I do!"

And of course, your BFF in high school always has your back and has your best interest in mind, so she says, "Then call Paul back and say YES! And then break up with your boyfriend! Duh!!!"

And that's what I did! I called Paul back in less than an hour and said, "Paul, I would love to go sailing with you if the offer is still open."

On a beautiful sunny day in March 1975, a seventeen-year-old girl and a nineteen-year-old boy sailed across the threshold of what would be a forty-year love affair. Five years later, on April 12, 1980, when Paul and I married, my BFF from high school was my maid of honor. Tab was Paul's best man, and his girlfriend, Terri (who was now his wife), was one of my bridesmaids. Our closest friends were with us from the start of our decades-long romance.

In high school, Paul was a good student. He could have been better academically, but his social activities were more important. Paul was a wrestling team member, ran cross country for the high school track team, and was a drummer in the marching band. Paul was also a Boy Scout—a fact he kept secret from most of his high school friends. He stayed with Scouting and earned the highest achievement possible in the BSA Scouting program, Eagle Scout. Only four percent of all Scouts in the program have received this honor since 1911. As an adult, Paul was proud of being an

Eagle Scout and occasionally sponsored young Scouts in the program. The values of leadership, perseverance, and discipline Paul learned during his Scouting years served him well as an entrepreneur. Paul also had a passion for surfing and spent his free time chasing the waves just off Huntington Beach's pier.

After high school graduation, Paul spent two years at a local junior college before transferring to UCLA as a junior. He was quickly accepted as a fraternity brother into the Beta Theta Pi Fraternity and moved into the fraternity house in the fall of 1975, taking full advantage of all that fraternity life had to offer. Graduating from UCLA in 1978 with a degree in economics, he was offered a job as a stockbroker with a well-known brokerage firm. The view from his office in Marina Del Rey, California, proved to be a bit too distracting while studying for his stockbroker license. He failed the test, and the company immediately fired him. Needing a job, Paul called his dad for help. Paul's dad had worked in the corrugated packaging industry for years and made a few phone calls to his colleagues and competitors. Within the week, Paul was offered a job as a salesman with Inland Container Corp., a large, corrugated mill in Los Angeles. Paul was paid nine hundred dollars a month and given a company car and benefits, and off he went.

Less than a year later, Paul and I married. Paul was almost twenty-five, and I had just turned twenty-three. After renting a 700-square-foot, one-bedroom apartment, Paul and I had less than two hundred dollars in the bank. Eighteen months later, with help from my parents, Paul and I bought our first home—a two-bedroom condo in Mission Viejo in August 1981. We welcomed our first son, Kris, in June 1982, our second son, Cory, in August 1986, and our daughter, Dani, in April 1989. Paul continued to work for the corrugated mill in Los Angeles during those years and earned top salesman distinction for several years.

In 1989, with three children under the age of seven and a mortgage, Paul came home one Friday evening and said, "I want to quit my job and start my own business. I've noticed most of my corrugated customers purchase labels, instruction sheets, and folding cartons, and I hear them complain about bad quality, high prices, long lead times, and poor customer service from their suppliers. I know I can fill that niche in Southern California."

The following Monday morning, Paul resigned and turned in the company car. He had a vision and a desire to own his own company, and he knew he could do it. And so did I. We had no idea what was involved in starting a manufacturing business, how much money and sweat equity it would require, and the stress it would produce. Good stress motivates you instead of paralyzing you. But stress, nonetheless.

I worked alongside Paul from the beginning as a non-paid employee, managing daily administrative details, like payables, receivables, and payroll. I prepared month-end reports and provided our accountant with our general ledger, trial balance, and supporting documents to prepare year-end financial reports. I worked closely with attorneys and insurance brokers to ensure the company was compliant with rules, regulations, and laws. Paul appreciated my support, and I was grateful that I only had to work a few days in the office. My number one job was being a mom, and I wanted to be available to participate in our kids' activities. Not many couples can successfully work together. But Paul and I made it work.

For the next nineteen years, we focused on raising our three children. We lived on a street named White Oaks in a neighborhood plucked right out of a Norman Rockwell painting. Twenty-two homes with beautifully manicured lawns on a quiet cul-de-sac in a gated community. Most of the forty-two children living on our street participated in the annual 4th of July street parade or Christmas caroling during the holidays. Friday nights during the summer months became a welcomed opportunity for neighbors to gather outside on driveways for dinner and conversation. As parents, Paul and I dove headfirst into all our kids' school activities and sports—baseball, football, wrestling, track, soccer, PTA, booster clubs, etc.

We wiped away tears after injuries on the field or following injuries of the heart over break-ups. We straddled the line between always providing a safety net for our kids and letting them fall and learn from their mistakes. We praised their achievements, whether big or small, and celebrated lessons learned from their challenges.

Along the way, we met our best friends on that street, in that neighborhood, and during those activities. The neighborhood kids and our children's friends called Paul "Mr. Paul, Coach Paul, or Papa G." And they called me "Miss Marci or Mama G." The first Christmas after Paul died, my daughter made me a special scrapbook. She reached out to some of the kids on our street, their parents, and family friends and asked them to write down one or two memories of Paul. These are precious, sweet, heartwarming memories that I will always treasure. Here is what some friends and neighbors thought of Papa G and the impact he made in their lives:

Diane - "My first memory of Paul was seeing him sitting on the side of the pool at 17. He was so good-looking. He was a surfer dude, a drummer in a band, a fun guy, someone who aggravated me and who I aggravated all the time. He became successful in business, even though it took time away from family events."

Lexi - "Mr. Paul was the 'cool and chill dad' on the street who was always riding his longboard and laughing. I'll never forget the many times he would be talking to my parents, stop and see me below them, and say how beautiful I was growing up to be. I'll never forget his laugh and inspiration as well as the many 4th of July parades he led on his skateboard with us kids trailing along behind him."

Christal - "Yes, Paul Glidden was one 'bitchen' guy. When the kids were young, Paul would let all the kids climb up and stand in the back of his truck. They thought he was so cool. And Paul was! He was so charismatic! I can just see him out in front of the house, washing his truck, or later down the road washing his kids' vehicles. Or it could have been a boat or some motorcycle out there too."

Nikki - "I have so many good memories of Paul. I've known him since I was three years old. He was an awesome big brother to me. One of the best memories is when he and my sister, Marci, went to see ZZ Top in concert. They came into the house at the end of the night laughing and still singing the show's songs. My sister busted out the air guitar as they walked inside the house. I smile every time I think about it."

Tab - "A friendship that spanned 40 years is hard to sum up in a few words. From crazy days (and nights) in college to starting our careers and businesses, to getting married and starting families to road trips, to spending hours together and on the phone as young men trying to figure things out. But I think the most important thing is that even as life took us in different directions, we could reconnect by just a phone call and pick up where we left off. More importantly, I knew that if I needed help, no matter if I was halfway around the world, Paul would have been there. A precious friendship that started with, "Hey, do you need a lab partner?""

Terri - "One of my fondest memories with Paul was when we were in Santa Fe, New Mexico. The four of us, Paul, Marci, Tab, and Terri, have gone to Santa Fe together several times. One time we were all in an elevator in a hotel, and we got stuck—it just stopped moving. I was about seven weeks pregnant, and Paul was so worried, and he kept yelling out to people, "we have a pregnant woman in here, and you need to get her out." So, by the time we got out, which wasn't too long, a crowd was outside watching the rescue and couldn't wait to see this pregnant girl get out. (At the time, I didn't look pregnant at all.) But Paul kept being the gentleman and wanted to get me out of there. He got me through the crowd and made sure I was okay. I loved those times in Santa Fe and will always have great memories with my dear friend. Paul - I love you and miss you.

Barb - "I loved Paul Glidden, and I look forward to seeing him in Heaven! After his dog, Tucker, died, Paul asked if he would see Tucker in Heaven. We talked about the Bible, stating that all things we loved would be in Heaven, and Tucker was one of his favorite beings (next to his family). Sometimes I picture them together and wonder what job God has him doing and what joy Paul has that we can't understand."

Teensy - "I was going through my divorce and barely holding it together. Paul was always full of funny off-color quips that would make me smile. However, on this one day, he told me, 'you're going to be okay. You're going to find happiness after this asshole!' He was right.

Cathy - "After we watched the sunset, ate burgers, and were hanging out, I said to Paul how much Danny really looked up to Cory and Kris, and despite moving away, he still talked about Paul and the boys all the time. I said that Danny wanted to get a pickup truck just like them when he got his license. That comment prompted Paul to sit up in his chair and say he needed to tell me the tricks and secrets—I felt like I was getting true insider info! Paul gave very sound advice: get a truck without a second seat so that you can limit how many kids are transported; make sure Danny knows he has to take care of the truck. After all, it can be taken away as fast as given, and get a fantastic color because those attract the pretty girls. I left that chat smiling to myself, thinking, Paul is one wise man—no wonder he raised boys that others want to emulate!!!"

Kerstin - "I remember Paul as the 'Bad Ass Dad' of White Oaks. I will never forget the Christmas party that Paul and Marci hosted when I went through cancer treatment. Paul was so protective, sensitive, and aware of my limitations; he made me comfortable during a challenging time. Most of all, I remember Paul as a man who adored his wife and kids beyond all else. Watching the two of them, Paul and Marci, from behind once, walking out of the movie theatre, not realizing it was them, they looked so young and in love, holding hands and strolling out of the theatre together. It was priceless preciousness."

Debbie - "Our sons fondly remember Paul because he was a business owner who made being home for his children a priority. Thus, the kids saw and interacted with Paul more than any other male parent in the neighborhood. Paul was a down-to-earth, straight-talking dad who played ball with the kids and generally related to them like no one else. He was always there for the kids— his or mine—or any other kid on the street."

Sheree - "I close my eyes, and I see Paul driving up in his truck with his '70s surfer' license plate thinking, what a cool dude! He is always so connected and involved with his kids, has an amazing relationship with you, and is a great neighbor. Paul loved our doggies so much that he needed to get one of his own. And he did—sweet Tucker. Oh, how Paul loved that dog! We remember when Tucker would get a bubble bath, and Paul would do the tennis ball "spin dry" in the street and then give him the big rubdown to remove all the loose hair! Cheering and moaning about UCLA football was an annual fall event. Our son has said several times that he misses Paul. As our son got older, he appreciated those talks and took Paul's insights about life to heart. I wish I had snapped a picture of them sitting around the fire pit at the Christmas party last year, deep in conversation. Later I asked my son, 'what on earth were you two talking about?' He simply said with a grin, 'stuff.'"

Kat - "We remember not one special thing but a thousand little things that made him such a kind, soulful, compassionate, and caring friend, neighbor, and human being. Not once or twice, but many times he would stop and take the time to talk to our kids about everything and anything, like how was their day, school, baseball, gymnastics? He would compliment them, praise them. They would come in from outside and say... 'Yeah, Mom... just talking to Mr. Paul.' Paul was a party starter. He had a smile that would light up the room, and he always said the funniest, impromptu snarky, sarcastic, hilarious quips, announcements, or comments. We referred to Paul and Marci as the Newlyweds. There was a naturally swirling energy of adoration surrounding them. You'd never know by the way they just looked at each other that they had been married for decades. My husband would say that the best part of being at a party with Paul is when all the guys would move the party to the backyard and sit around just being guys. Jim and I were talking about Paul recently, and he reminded me of the season where Paul started a men's small group with the White Oaks guys to fellowship and study God's word. He is the coolest guy that we know, being a witness to the love of Christ and sharing God's word with his buddies. Awesome! At the right time, we will all meet again, and we will count on him to make us laugh till we cry and to get the party started."

Dan - "I have many fond memories of Paul. Some are simple; some are complex. They span from watching Tucker taking Paul for a walk to backyard kibitzing and talking about the politics of the day. The memory that stands first in my mind, both chronologically and emotionally, is the 4th of July. That was the day Paul played the Pied Piper of White Oaks. Paul didn't have a magic flute, yet he held some mystical sway over the local munchkins. Every Fourth, Paul, leading the 4th of July parade as if he was MacArthur returning to the Philippines, or Washington crossing the Delaware, or Napoleon through the Arc Triomphe (okay, now I am exaggerating). In 1998, my virtual introduction to the varied and lasting friendships we would make over the next few years. There stands Paul. Barefoot, flag taped to the kick-tail of his skateboard. Smiling."

Kathy T. - "Paul just had a way of making everyone happy. Our boating days were a time of waiting forever on the dock for our pilot to be ready to go, sweating. At the same time, we waited, lugging more stuff than any of us needed, sand in everything, jet skis that always required some tinkering, the 'Safety Talk,' perfect ski coves, chick rides, cliff jumping, matchbox cars, cigars, Cheez Whiz, cold beer, wine coolers, windy rides back to the dock, and those ugly carp waiting for our return. But what I remember most was laughter! Paul always made sure we had plenty of laughter!"

Donna - "Papa G was all about boating and skiing. I began having knee issues, but that didn't keep me from water skiing. I just brought duct tape with me and taped my knees straight. You don't know Papa G if you think he let that go without notice or comment. That was the beginning of our 'tease' and 'taunt' friendship. Papa G listened about my heartbreak and a broken marriage. I will always remember him coming to my house after the settlement decisions were over and telling me 'you can do this.' You are in great shape. I believed him, and he was right. Papa G comes to mind every day, and I am reminded of how much I miss his humor, wit, ability to identify my sore spots, get to the core of the issue, and assure me that God loves me. Even though Papa G had his special daughter, he made time for my daughter, Mandy; there is nothing more special in my heart than that. I am forever thankful and blessed to know him as my friend."

Mandy - "There are so many things I could say and memories I could share about Papa G...one of my favorite things is he loved to have little chats. They were his forte. He always pulled me aside whenever I was having a tough day, suffering over my multiple break-ups and anything in-between. When I went through my first break-up in high school, and things got ugly, Papa G was there to intervene. It was the first time I felt like a man had ever protected me. Papa G came over (after telling the particular boyfriend never to contact me again and keep his hands off his daughter) to have a little chat telling me that it would be okay, and there would be MANY boyfriends to follow. Although it was hard for me to imagine at the time, I knew that Papa G had my back. Another memorable chat happened when I was contemplating going to Tennessee for graduate school, and it was wearing on me physically and emotionally. Well, Papa G picked up that I was struggling during a Mother's Day brunch. He looked at me, pointed his finger, and said, 'let's take a walk outside.' We sat down next to a tree with purple flowers and went through the pros and cons. As we sat on a ledge pulling apart the little flowers that had fallen, discussing a plan, I can remember so vividly thinking how fortunate I was to have Papa G love and support me. Papa G was the ultimate example of love. Not only did he love his gorgeous family unconditionally, but also those close to him. I will never forget how he (and you too, Mama G) took me into the family with open arms and never let me go."

Monica - "I have so many memories of Paul that I couldn't possibly list them all here. The thing that always comes to mind is when he would stop by our house on the way home from work to have a beer with Marc. He knew he didn't have to ask for one—he just went to the fridge in the garage and grabbed one on the way into the house. Marc and Paul would sit at the kitchen table and talk business, fire department, and kids. Soon he would say, 'gotta go. Marci has dinner ready.' And he would be off speeding down the street! We will forever miss those visits."

Marc (aka Hawk) - "I first met Paul when our boys played little league baseball 22 years ago. I first noticed Marci because she was hot, and there was this guy, her husband, with a mullet and an exploding personality. Once introductions were made, we became fast friends. Soon we started going on family vacations together at Lake Mohave and Laughlin. The river is not the same without Paul. I miss us scouting out new Glidden coves on the jet skis for him and Marci. I miss going to concerts, acting like fools on the beach, smoking cigars, drumming on the dashboard to Boston, getting crazy over politics, and his cheese enchiladas and Coors Light. I enjoyed the times Paul would stop by our house for a beer on the way home from work. He was comfortable coming in through the garage after grabbing two beers from the fridge for us. His limit was always two when he'd say, 'gotta get home to Marci.' I miss my friend. What I don't miss is his constant obsession with work. The last time I saw Paul, we met for lunch. We sat down and ordered lunch and a beer. Then his damn phone rang, and he said, 'gotta go' after only 20 minutes. Again, work was calling. He could never get away from it."

And I will never forget the night that one of the neighborhood kids knocked on our door around 1:00 am. He needed money because he had gotten into some trouble and couldn't tell his parents. Paul gave him the money. No questions asked, and no expectation of ever being repaid. Years passed, and one day out of the blue, that boy who had grown up appeared at our door again and paid Paul back the money he had borrowed years earlier."

I don't think Paul ever knew how many people admired him and loved him outside of his own family. These memories show what an ordinary and extraordinary man our Paul Glidden was. He had a formidable and treasonous opponent. Its power depended on silence. No more.

CHAPTER 3

What Lies Beneath

"The tragedy of life is in what dies inside a man while he lives." [1]
—Norman Cousins

It's true. Paul had a tough time getting away from work because the buck stopped with him. Every decision he made, like purchasing equipment for our manufacturing facility, hiring a General Manager, generating sales, managing inventory at levels not to impede cash flow, and understanding our customers' packaging needs, directly affected the business. No sales teams were helping grow our business. No human resource department to manage employee problems. No private equity firm or silent partners to provide funding during months of slow sales. Times of economic instability, the emergence of new competitors, foreign and domestic, and changing legislation can significantly affect a business's bottom line. Owning your own business can be stressful, but it also provides the freedom to make decisions and reap your hard work rewards. That's what Paul signed up for the day he decided to start his company.

Like so many men, Paul wanted to provide for his family the best he could. Paul grew up watching his father, Howard (a.k.a. Bud), excel as a salesman for a large paper mill in Southern California until Bud had his first heart attack. When Bud returned to work after recuperating, the company demoted Bud to an inside sales service representative providing sales support and customer service support to the outside sales force. The demotion was devastating for Bud. Paul related his dad's story to the Willie Lohmann character in Arthur Miller's "Death of a Salesman." I believe Bud's demotion was the pivotal moment when Paul knew he didn't ever want to work for someone that could yield that much control over his career.

PAUL'S FATHER DIES

In 1981, Paul worked two blocks from his dad's office in Los Angeles. On September 29, Paul left his office at the end of the workday and noticed his dad's green Volkswagen stopped in the middle of the first intersection surrounded by paramedics. Paul pulled over his car, jumped out, and ran to the corner. Bud was lying in the street, eyes open and glazed over while paramedics administered CPR. Paul wasn't sure if his dad was dead or alive. The paramedics continued life-saving measures as they placed Bud on a gurney and loaded him into the ambulance. Traumatized and in shock, Paul followed the ambulance to the local hospital, where doctors put Bud on life support. Within a few hours, my mother-in-law, sisters-in-law, and I joined Paul at the hospital, and together we huddled in a small waiting room, anxiously waiting for news from the doctors. Subsequent tests confirmed the family's biggest fear—Bud lost too much oxygen between the time he slumped over at the wheel of his car and when paramedics arrived. And there was no detectable brain activity. A few days later, my mother-in-law gathered the family at her home to discuss the devastating option of removing Bud from life support. With no brain activity and no chance of ever waking from the coma, the family agreed to remove Bud from all life-sustaining equipment. The medical staff allowed each family member as much time as needed, alone with Bud, before shutting down the machines.

Surprisingly, Bud's heart continued to beat for another sixteen days. Bud passed away on October 15, 1981, the same day I found out I was pregnant with our first child. As I left the obstetrician's office, Paul called to tell me his dad passed, and he was on his way to his mom's house. I said I would meet him there as soon as I could. As I drove to my mother-in-law's house, I worried about what to say to Paul if he asked me about my doctor's appointment. Paul knew why I was going to the doctor. Do I tell Paul I missed my doctor's appointment, or do I tell him the truth? How do I tell my husband he's going to be a dad on the same day his father died? When I arrived, the first question Paul asked was, "Am I going to be a dad?" I said, "Yes, you are!" Paul always told me I did the right thing that day by telling him I was pregnant. Knowing he was going to be a father helped Paul deal with his father's death.

Paul was twenty-six when his dad died. I don't know if my mother-in-law or sisters-in-law ever received any type of grief counseling after Bud's death, but I know Paul didn't. Paul did what many men do, ignored his grief, and showed little emotion, if at all. I wish Paul and I were older and knew how vital grief counseling could have been. Paul lived with his dad's traumatic image lying in that intersection for the rest of his life.

DISRUPTIVE SLEEP - MEDICATION PRESCRIBED

For years, Paul experienced disruptive sleep patterns, difficulty falling asleep, and staying asleep. Paul struggled, turning off the "replay tape of the day" in his mind. Thoughts kept him awake, like a hamster on a wheel that keeps going around and around. In hopes of getting Paul the needed and necessary sleep, a doctor prescribed a sleeping aid. The first sleeping medication Paul was prescribed produced dangerous side effects, such as sleepwalking and memory loss. Paul would drive to the store late at night for ice cream and not remember doing so, or we could engage in "adult extracurricular activities" after the kids were asleep and Paul would not remember the following day. Our kids thought it was funny and joked among themselves that, "If you want something...ask Dad after he's taken his medicine."

After finding a sleep medication that didn't produce dangerous side effects, Paul still did not get revitalizing sleep and felt tired most of the time. So, the doctor ordered Paul to take a sleep study. After less than an hour into the study, it was clear that Paul had sleep apnea—a potentially dangerous sleep disorder where Paul's breathing would start and stop many times during the night. The constant disruption in breathing wasn't allowing Paul to get restful and uninterrupted sleep. Once Paul received a CPAP machine, he struggled with wearing the mask. He complained to the doctor and said he couldn't fall asleep with the plastic mask without a sleeping pill. It seemed Paul became more dependent on his sleep medication once he was given a CPAP machine for his sleep apnea. Sleep disorders can sometimes lead to self-medicating with drugs or alcohol.

MORE MEDICATION PRESCRIBED - AN SSRI

Not long after Paul received his CPAP machine, his doctor prescribed Paul a well-known anti-anxiety/antidepressant drug to help with his sleep and hopefully boost his energy level. The combination of the SSRI, sleeping pill, and CPAP machine seemed to work...at least for a while. Or maybe it appeared to be working for everyone except Paul.

2007 AND THE HOUSING MARKET CRASH

We sold our house on White Oaks and bought a newer home in a nearby community. You've heard the saying, "Timing is everything"? A few months after we moved into our new home, the housing market crashed due to the subprime crisis. The house we purchased lost significant equity. By the end of 2007, our home's value dropped a half-million dollars less than we paid for the place six months earlier—three of the twelve homes on our small cul-de-sac short sold. Even though the real estate market tanked, we planned on staying in the house for ten or more years and believed the market would eventually turn around.

FEBRUARY 2008 - AN ATTEMPT

We planned a three-day weekend skiing trip over President's Day weekend in February 2008. Paul and our oldest son, Kris, would ski or snowboard while I enjoyed a little "retail therapy." I tried skiing twice before but failed miserably to understand why skiing was the least bit fun. It had been a while since Paul had skied, so he needed to rent skis and boots. On Wednesday, February 20, Paul left the office early to pick up the rentals and start packing. When I got home around 4:30 that afternoon, I went upstairs to say hello to Paul and see how the packing was going, but he was napping. Not unusual. Paul would often rest for thirty to forty-five minutes at the end of a workday.

I went back downstairs to make a glass of iced tea, and as I opened the refrigerator, I got a bizarre, unsettling feeling and could have sworn I heard a faint voice say, "Go check the bottle." What? Check the bottle? Before I processed my next thought, I ran up the stairs to the bathroom to look for Paul's bottle of sleeping pills. Found it, and it was empty. I checked the date it was filled and started to panic. The container shouldn't be empty. Oh, God, what has he done?

I tried to wake him, but he seemed so tired and slurred his speech. I tried pulling on his arms to get him to sit up in bed, but he wouldn't. He kept mumbling that he was sleepy. Our son, Cory, lived in our casita at the time, so I called him from my cell phone and told him to come upstairs quickly because I needed his help with Dad. With Cory holding Paul up on one side and me on the other, we got him out of bed; Paul stumbled and almost fell. We decided it was best not to walk him down the stairs but sit him back in bed. Cory stayed with him while I ran downstairs to call the doctor who prescribed the sleeping pills.

I told our doctor I thought Paul had taken ten or so sleeping pills, and we were having a hard time getting him to wake up. The doctor thought Paul had not taken enough to be fatal but enough to make him sleep for quite a while. He said it was a good idea to get Paul out of bed and at least try to communicate. By describing his behavior, the doctor did not think Paul was in any immediate danger of dying, but I would need to monitor him through the next hours continually, or I could call 911 for help now. When I got off the phone and went back upstairs, Paul seemed to be a little more coherent and talked about how he didn't know what happened, but he remembered trying to throw up. He kept saying it was like an out-of-body experience. I couldn't believe what I heard, much less the fact that my husband had almost overdosed. Oh, God, what do I do?

I called one of our friends, who happened to be a chaplain. Paul and I had been in a couples' Bible study group with the chaplain and his wife, and we knew them for years. They were at our house within twenty minutes of my phone call. The chaplain went upstairs to talk to Paul and assess what happened, while his wife stayed downstairs with me. After talking with Paul for a while, the chaplain returned downstairs and said he believed this was not an accident but a suicide attempt. Suicide attempt??? I stood in the kitchen, tears rolling down my face, slowly shaking my head in disagreement and utter disbelief. I realized the seriousness of what happened, and I needed to get help for Paul. I picked up the phone, dialed 911, and told the operator my husband had swallowed half a bottle of sleeping pills and I needed help.

Paramedics and sheriffs arrived at our house within minutes. After assessing Paul medically and questioning me, everyone agreed Paul needed further evaluation at the local hospital. Before I left, I asked Cory to call his brother Kris and tell him to meet me at the hospital. I also requested Cory and his wife, Erin, to drive to San Diego to pick up our daughter and bring her to the hospital.

The paramedics would not let me ride in the back with Paul; they had me ride upfront with the driver. The seven-minute ride to the hospital felt like an hour. Once we arrived, they promptly whisked Paul through the double doors and down the hallway. The hospital staff directed me to an office to fill out the necessary paperwork, provide a health insurance card, answer medical history questions about Paul, and sign on his behalf. After I finished and the medical staff had completed their initial assessment, I was allowed to see him.

As much as I wanted to deny what happened, reality hit when I saw a police officer standing guard outside of Paul's ER room, hospital protocol when they admit someone for a suicide attempt. Paul was lying on the hospital bed on his side, facing the wall, when I walked into the room. I leaned down and kissed him on the forehead, but no response. I wasn't sure if he was asleep or avoiding me. The nurse came into the room and told me it would be several more hours before Paul would have a psych evaluation, so she suggested I go home and get some sleep for a few hours and regroup.

By this time, all my kids were in the hospital waiting room, along with the chaplain and his wife. I told the kids the doctors would keep their dad overnight, and we wouldn't know anything until the morning. I assured them that their dad was okay. I also told them I couldn't believe this was intentional, and there must be a reasonable explanation or reason—no need to worry. Everything would be okay, whether I believed that or not was another question. I decided to go home and rest for a few hours and return in the morning.

I don't remember all the details of the next twelve to sixteen hours, but I remember vividly the decision I had to make when I returned to the hospital the following morning. A guard still stood outside Paul's ER Room, and Paul was still lying on his side toward the wall. I tried again to talk to Paul, tell him how much I loved him and how much the kids loved him. Hoping and praying that he was hearing my heart and not just my words. A few minutes later, the psychiatrist came into the room, introduced herself, and sat in the chair across from me. After her preliminary assessment, she told me Paul admitted to being under a great deal of stress, particularly over an email he had received from someone who owed him money and couldn't pay. Paul also told her the only way he could explain what happened was that it felt like an out-of-body experience, and when he realized he had swallowed all the pills, Paul tried to throw up, but he couldn't.

I waited for her to say the magic words, "Mrs. Glidden, I don't believe this was a suicide attempt. I'll adjust Paul's current medications to reduce his anxiety, and he should feel much better in a few days." Instead, she said, "After evaluating Paul, I don't believe he is in danger of hurting himself in the short-term, and so I will release him into your care." I thought, not in the short term? Release him to me? The other alternative she suggested was to place Paul on an involuntary 51/50 hold for seventy-two hours. The hospital would transport him to the Behavioral Health Inpatient Department at St. Joseph Hospital for further evaluation. It was my decision.

I would have done anything to save Paul's life, including making the hardest decision I ever had to make in our marriage when I signed the papers to place him on a 51/50 and have him transferred to a psych ward. I was scared, but I knew he needed help. I did what I thought was best for him and our family. I did what I had to do. The doctor told me exactly where they were taking Paul, what I needed to pack for him, and what I couldn't bring (like a belt, hooded sweatshirt with a drawstring), and what time the limited visiting hours were. Paul got up off the bed without saying a word, walked out of the ER room, got on the gurney waiting for him in the hallway, and off he went. Why didn't Paul say something to me? Was he mad at me? Was he embarrassed? I second-guessed myself the rest of the day.

Visiting hours for the Behavioral Health Unit at St. Joseph's were only one hour in the evenings, and it was up to the patient to decide who they did or did not want to see. The kids and I drove to the hospital that evening, not knowing what to expect. I was the first one allowed to see Paul and bring him his bag of clothes, toothbrush, etc. Each door I walked through locked behind me. Just outside the final entry to the patient rooms was a chair. The hospital staff asked me to sit in the chair and wait until Paul was ready to see me. The double doors next to the chair had windows to see the comings and goings of patients and staff. At one point, I saw Paul come out of a room and start walking with other patients in the opposite direction from the door I was sitting nearby. A nurse walked by, noticed my look of confusion, and explained it was time for a designated "smoke break" for patients who smoked. Twelve years later, I can still see Paul walking down the hall with other patients in my mind's eye, and I remember thinking that my husband doesn't belong here.

Paul returned from his smoke break and walked down the hall-way toward me. The visiting room for patients and families was small and crowded with no privacy. Paul and I sat down on one of the couches, hugged, and talked. Paul was tearful and repeatedly said he didn't know what happened, and he wasn't trying to kill himself. He promised! Paul was desperate for me to believe him. I told him the kids were waiting down the hall, and they wanted to see him, but he said no! He was embarrassed and did not want his children to see him in this place. I understood because deep down inside of me, I also didn't want them to see their dad this way and in this place. Not ever.

After the allowed half-hour visit, we kissed, I told him I loved him, and I would be back in the morning. It was tough to leave him after I had seen the stark reality of this unit. I tried to explain to the kids why he didn't want to see them while he was in the hospital. I know they were disappointed, but I also think they were a little relieved. Like me, they couldn't believe their "Superhero, Cool Dad" was in a psych ward. Maybe if they didn't see him here, they could pretend it never happened.

As promised, I returned the following day for visiting hours. But this time, one of the nurses led me through the locked door into a large room with several round tables and chairs, like a classroom or a room used for more extensive group therapy. Paul joined me there after a few minutes. We were the only ones in the room, and I was thankful for the privacy. Paul had a session earlier in the morning with a psychiatrist who advised Paul to be open and honest with me. Paul told me he had been taking narcotic pain medication for a while and hiding his usage from me. I felt blindsided. I asked him why he lied to me, but more importantly, why was he taking pain meds? He turned toward me and said, "They make me feel like I can do anything!"

The hospital released Paul in forty-eight hours, and by week's end, we were sitting in a psychiatrist's office. Over the following weeks and months, I went with Paul to his psychiatry appointments. The psychiatrist would see me first for about ten or fifteen minutes to describe my observations of Paul's behavior at home and his overall mood. I am not aware that Paul was officially diagnosed with depression. Paul did not talk to me about his sessions with the psychiatrist. I don't think Paul ever wanted to admit to himself or anyone else that he was struggling. I gave Paul a journal and encouraged him to write down his feelings and share them with his doctor. I never knew if or what he ever wrote in the journal because I never read it until after he died in August 2014.

I was terrified of the number of different medications the psychiatrist prescribed for Paul to take daily, and Paul knew it. Paul insisted I be the medicines' gatekeeper, so I always knew when and how much he was taking. Periodically, the doctor adjusted Paul's medications, and we never knew what side effects would pop up, good or bad. After about six months, Paul felt like he was okay and decided to stop seeing the psychiatrist. And on the outside, Paul appeared to be back to his usual self.

CUSTOMERS GO BANKRUPT, AND PAUL'S PARTNER WANTS OUT

During this time, one of our customers closed their doors overnight, and another customer sold their business to a foreign investor who stripped the company of cash and assets before selling the brand. The financial hit to our business was close to $250,000. Paul and his partner needed to personally invest more money into the company due to these losses, so Paul flew to our manufacturing facility in Texas to discuss the options with his partner. Paul was surprised and disappointed when his partner refused to invest more capital into the company. His partner wanted out of our company immediately and demanded they reach an agreement on a fair buyout. The timing couldn't have been worse.

Throughout our company's history, we always paid our vendors in total, and this time was no exception. We paid for all the products we shipped to the customers who never paid us. We also agreed to a buyout agreement over the next three years with our partner in Texas. Our business was now strapped for cash and needed to borrow money to keep the doors open. It was a very stressful time, but Paul remained optimistic and believed he could keep the ship righted. He did, but the stress took a toll on his physical and emotional health.

FEBRUARY 2010 – PROSTATE CANCER

At the age of fifty-four, Paul learned he had an aggressive form of prostate cancer. Two weeks following the diagnosis, surgeons at the City of Hope Comprehensive Cancer Center in Duarte, California, successfully removed Paul's prostate using the da Vinci Surgical System. Paul and I celebrated the great news; Paul was cancer-free, and he would not need chemotherapy or radiation. Seventy-two hours post-surgery, Paul's surgeon discharged him from the hospital with instructions to follow up every six months with his urologist. That was it—no heads up about the challenges going forward or the possibility of any side effects, including depression.

The road to recovery following prostate cancer can be physically challenging and intensely emotional. The after-effects of prostate cancer required Paul and me to find a new normal for the most intimate part of our marriage. We didn't shy away from couples' therapy, seeking advice and suggestions from other prostate cancer survivors to redefine sexual intimacy in our marriage. Together we committed to finding what worked best for us.

2011 TO 2013

By 2011, all three of our children had graduated from college. We completed paying eleven consecutive years of college tuition, books, and housing payments. Paul worked hard to provide each of our kids with the gift of graduating from college debt-free. Our oldest son, Kris, met Kelley, a wonderful woman who would become our second daughter-in-law, in February 2014. Cory, our youngest son, married Erin, the love of his life, in July 2011, and two years later, in 2013, gave us our first grandson—Colt Grayson Glidden.

In November 2013, our oldest son, Kris, age 31, took a minor spill on his motorcycle while riding in the desert with family and friends near our vacation home in Lake Havasu. Kris sustained some scrapes and cuts and a bruised ego, but no broken bones or any injury that required medical attention. That's what we thought. Five days later, his fiancée Kelley (now his wife) found Kris unconscious and barely breathing. After calling the paramedics, Kelley called us and told us we needed to meet her at the hospital as quickly as possible. By the time Paul and I arrived at the ER, Kris was intubated and lying in a coma.

Kris lay in a coma for two and a half days in intensive care while a team of doctors put him through a battery of tests to determine what was wrong. We weren't sure he would survive until doctors finally found the five pulmonary embolisms in his lung and knew how to treat him. Paul's family and all three of our children are carriers of a blood-clotting gene. Watching your son lie motionless in a coma, teetering between life and death, is a parent's worst nightmare. A few days before Thanksgiving, the doctors released Kris from the hospital. On Thanksgiving Day, the immediate family came to our home to celebrate and offer thanks for Kris's recovery. With the family gathered around the table, heads bowed and holding hands, Paul began the prayer. After a few short words, Paul was overcome with emotion and collapsed on the dining room table crying.

2014

2014 looked like it would be a good and successful year. Both of our sons were active in our business and eager to take it over one day, which had always been Paul's goal and dream. At our fiscal year-end in June, our company showed the most significant sales and growth in its twenty-five-year history, allowing Paul and me to start making plans for a three to five-year exit strategy from the company's daily operations. The dream and reality of retirement were on the horizon.

In late June 2014, our daughter's boyfriend, Mike, showed up at our house with a "ring" in hand and asked Paul for Dani's hand in marriage.

It was traditional, respectful, and what Paul expected from the man who would marry his baby girl. They talked man-to-man for a few minutes before inviting me to join them. Lots of joyful tears and discussions of an engagement party to plan! After Mike left our house, I remember Paul saying, "I better start working on my speech now. I want it to be the best speech ever." A few weeks later, Mike pulled off a "surprise proposal and surprise engagement party with a little help." Over eighty friends and family celebrated the newly engaged couple at our home. It was a wonderful evening of celebration, topped off with a heartfelt prayer and speech from the "father of the bride." That would be the last night Dani saw her dad.

CHAPTER 4

August 13, 2014

"The greater the love, the greater the tragedy when it's over." [1]
—Nicholas Sparks

Friday, August 8, 2014 – I treated Paul to a surprise massage at a local spa. We grabbed dinner afterward, went home, and had "run around the house naked" fun—culminating in awesome, intimate, crazy-good SEX!

Saturday, August 9, 2014 – We babysat our sixteen-month-old grandson, Colt. As proud grandparents often do, Paul and I wanted to spoil Colt with a new toy, so we took him to the Disney store in our local mall. The last photo ever taken of Paul was with Colt in the Disney store, watching a video. We had dinner at a kid-friendly restaurant in the mall so that Colt could have his favorite meal, mac and cheese. After dinner, we took Colt back to our house for a sleepover.

Sunday, August 10, 2014 – Paul surprised me with tickets to see Miranda Lambert in concert. We had terrific seats six rows from the stage. Halfway through the show, a younger couple sitting next to me leaned over and asked, "How do you do it?"

I said, "How do we do what?"

The young man said, "Stay in love for a long time? We don't know you, but it's apparent that you two are crazy in love!"

Paul reached for my hand, we smiled at each other, and I said to the couple, "That's nice of you to say because we've been married for over thirty-four years. How do we do it? We never fall out of love on the same day."

Monday, August 11, 2014 – CNN breaking news: Robin Williams died of an apparent suicide.

Wednesday, August 13, 2014 – It was a very stressful morning at the office. Paul and Kris drove to L.A. to speak with a customer about some outstanding invoices they owed us. This customer had a history of not paying for products we sold them when under different management. The customer needed more products from us, but we held the order until we received a check in payment for the invoices over ninety days. Paul and Kris met with the company's owner and the new buyer, but they could not reach an agreement beneficial to both parties. When Paul and Kris returned to the office, Paul contacted our corporate attorney to discuss our options.

Our options were limited, and our attorney reminded us of the costs of pursuing a legal remedy. He suggested we would be "throwing good money after bad" and recommended we take the loss and move on. Around 1:30 p.m., Paul said he had a meeting with the buyer of one of our largest customers and hurried out the door. I remember watching Paul walk to his car and thinking Paul needed a haircut. Ironically, after Paul left the office, the customer who Paul and Kris had seen earlier in the morning called and said they issued payment in the amount Paul requested, and the check would be ready for pickup in the morning if we released the product to them. I immediately called Paul on his cell phone and asked him how he wanted me to respond to the customer.

Speaking in a low voice like he was in a meeting, Paul whispered, "That's great, baby. Release the product." I didn't know those were the last words I would hear Paul ever say.

Before I left the office around 4:30, I called Paul again on his cell phone to let him know I was on my way home, but he didn't answer. I stopped by a little Mexican food restaurant a block from the office to pick up chips and guacamole to go with our dinner and headed home. Fifteen to twenty minutes later, I turned onto our street and saw Paul's car in the driveway and the garage door open. I remember thinking Paul must have gotten home a few minutes before me and didn't shut the garage door because he knew I was on my way home. I pulled my car into the garage and parked. I grabbed my purse and the food and walked toward the door into the house.

As I entered the house, I noticed it was hushed. I didn't hear a television on, and our dog wasn't barking as he usually did. So, I thought Paul must be taking a nap upstairs. As I walked into the kitchen, out of the corner of my eye, I noticed the sliding glass door to our backyard was open about six inches, and I could see Paul's foot resting on the ottoman outside. I put the bag of food, my purse, and keys on the counter and walked to the sliding glass door to say, "I'm home, honey," expecting to sit down with my husband and discuss the day's events as we had done thousands of times before.

It's interesting how quickly your brain reacts to a fight, flight, or freeze response and prepares you to act without conscious thought when you witness a traumatic event. As I opened the sliding glass door and stepped outside onto the patio, I saw Paul sitting in the patio chair he always sat in, and our yellow lab sitting next to him. I thought how tired Paul must have been when he got home because he'd fallen asleep in the chair. But before I could finish that thought, I noticed blood on the right side of his head.

Oh no, Paul's hurt. What happened? And then I saw a handgun lying in the palm of his right hand that had fallen to his side. GUN? BLOOD? The surge of adrenaline my brain released clouded my mind, so it took a second to realize what I was seeing and what Paul had done. I couldn't catch my breath. I tried to scream, but my voice was frozen, and nothing came out. I moved toward him and touched his face. He was so cold, and he wasn't breathing. Oh my God, he's dead! I could hear myself saying NO! NO! NO! Oh, God - No!!!

I stumbled back into the house to grab the phone, but I was shaking so much it was hard to dial 911. I don't remember what I said, but I was crying and begging for someone to get here as quickly as possible. The dispatcher told me to go to the front of the house and wait for sheriffs to arrive. With the phone still in my hand, I ran to the garage screaming for someone to help me, but no one heard my cries. When the sheriffs arrived, they found me crying hysterically on the garage floor, in-between two cars. They asked me where my husband was, and I told them on the patio in the backyard. I also told the sheriffs I had a yellow lab that could be very protective of me and might start barking when he saw them. They had me enter the house in front of them to grab my dog and put him on a leash as they followed behind me. They asked me if anyone else could be in the house, and I said no because we lived alone. The sheriffs told me to sit in the dining room and wait. Before the sheriffs went to the backyard, they searched the house, holding their guns by their sides. Within minutes, fire-fighters and paramedics arrived, each one glancing at me as they entered the house.

Two female TIP (Trauma Intervention Program) volunteers arrived a few minutes later. They were on the scene to provide help and support for me following a traumatic death. A sheriff eventually sat down at the table with me to ask me questions for his report—what time I got home, what did I see, was anyone else at home, my husband's name, age, and on and on. Everyone around me seemed to move in slow motion. I couldn't hear their conversations over the sound of my heart beating. Thoughts popped in and out of my mind so quickly I couldn't focus. I don't know how long I sat at the table before realizing I had to call my kids. "Oh God… my kids… my kids, my kids. I can't do this." How do I tell my kids their dad is dead? And he shot himself. I couldn't protect them from this horrifying truth, and I couldn't fix it. The only control I had that day was keeping my kids from seeing Paul dead in the backyard and having it be the last image of their dad. Reliving that moment sucks the breath out of me and makes me nauseous to this very day.

Kris, Cory, and Dani arrived separately. Cory lived only two miles from our house, so he came first, followed by Kris and Dani. I didn't have to say a word to them. They took one look at my tear-stained face and knew they were walking into something so horrible it would change everything. I will never forget how their crying ebbed and flowed; screams slowly evaporated into silent gasps of air, as if with each cry, they heard the news all over, again and again. I fell to the floor with each of them, holding their shaking bodies and saying, "I'm so sorry!"

CHAPTER 5

When Everything Familiar Goes Missing

"When there is an undoing of your life, there is an unknowing of every next millisecond. Every next breath. The peaceful predictability of what you thought would be your life is suddenly replaced by very unexpected darkness and silence you aren't used to."[1]

—Lysa Terkeurst

H. Norman Wright explains the endless conversations in my mind in his book, *Experiencing Grief*: "Your mind fluctuates from being blank to thinking again and again about the one you lost. They come to mind hundreds of times a day, and it feels as though your mind is talking."[2]

Less than two hours after finding Paul dead, my courtyard was full of family and friends. They stood shoulder to shoulder, some crying and some talking. Others stood in silence and disbelief, trying to grasp the gravity of what happened and why. Paul dead? How could it be? No one knew what to do or what to say. And neither did I. My heart was racing. I felt an uneasy and foreboding feeling I had never felt before. I felt scared, vulnerable, and unprepared for the task at hand—getting through the first hours of my life without Paul.

No one was allowed in the house or the backyard while the coroner, sheriffs, and first responders were there except for one TIP volunteer and me. Even though I could be in the house, I didn't want to be within the eyesight of the crime scene. I also didn't want to be in my courtyard. At that moment, rational and logical thoughts went missing, keeping me from understanding that everyone standing in the courtyard was there because they loved me; they loved Paul and wanted to help. I see that now. But at the time, I felt like I was on display, and everyone had a front seat to my private anguish and pain. Rightly or wrongly, I started imagining the questions at the center of each conversation among my family and friends. I failed the man I loved by allowing his tragic death to be exposed and subjected to speculation and judgment. I wanted to scream, *"Paul didn't mean to do this. Please don't think less of him or blame him for this."*

I wanted to run and hide. I wanted to be alone to have a cigarette and feel the adrenaline kick the tobacco produced. I tried to reboot my mind so the rapid succession of thoughts could take a time-out. I wanted to talk to my inner self and *"remind her she was not alone. Remind her Paul's suicide was not her fault. Remind her she can survive."* The court-yard opened up to a large side yard on the right side of the house. It wasn't private, but I could sit in the grass, have the cigarette I craved, and think about what I needed to do next. I was sitting on the grass when my friend Sheree arrived. She ran toward me as though she couldn't reach me quickly enough and fell to the ground next to me. She held me as we both cried— the first of many times to follow.

When the coroner finished the investigation, she asked me to come into the house to talk with her. As I sat on the couch waiting, I noticed a young sheriff standing near the patio door with tears in his eyes. It could have been his first time dealing with suicide. I could sense that he wanted to hug me or say something about my loss, but he couldn't, so he did the next best thing. He reached into his pocket, pulled out some Mentos, and asked me if I wanted one. His simple gesture meant so much to me. At a time when words were insufficient, leaning in and acknowledging my pain and loss was all I could embrace. One week later, we passed out Mentos to everyone who attended Paul's memorial service in honor of that young, compassionate sheriff.

A few minutes later, the coroner sat down on the couch next to me. She asked me only one question, "Was Paul left- or right-handed?" Without hesitation, I said, "Right-handed." I felt like I was suddenly on an episode of Investigation Discovery or Dateline. I thought, Wow, she had to ask me that question because I was the only one home when the sheriffs arrived. Did anyone doubt it was a suicide? I asked her if Paul had left a note. She said no and handed me Paul's wedding ring, watch, and wallet. Symbols of what was left of almost forty years of my life lying in the palm of my hand. The wedding ring I had slipped on his finger thirty-four years earlier was now back in my custody. No longer a symbol of hopes and dreams for our future together, but a grim reminder of "until death do us part."

In a minute or so, I heard the coroner say, "We've prepared Paul for you to see him and say good-bye." I froze at the patio door and started crying again when I first saw him. Paul was lying on a gurney in a body bag, fully covered except for his face. I stepped toward him and noticed a couple of the coroner's assistants standing just past the gurney. Respectfully, they stood with heads bowed, gloved hands clasped behind their backs. I stood next to the gurney looking at Paul for a few minutes—thinking of that cute surfer boy I fell in love with so many years before. Then I leaned down and whispered in Paul's ear, "I love you, Paul, and I forgive you." I ran my fingers through his hair a few times and then leaned down, touched his bloody face, and kissed him one last time. My final physical moment with my beloved.

Once the coroner left, the sheriffs allowed family and friends in the house. I don't know what time it was or who was still there. My body was on autopilot, going through the motions on its own; while my mind was replaying and reliving the moment, I found him. I couldn't stop it. Every time I tried to shut my eyes, all I saw was Paul, the blood, and the gun. Maybe I was hoping if I replayed the events enough times, I could find a way to change the outcome so I could end this nightmare. But you can't escape reality.

Late in the evening, the phone rang. It was a donor procurement agency representative because Paul had a donor sticker on his driver's license. To proceed with organ or tissue donation, they needed Paul's medical history. Are you kidding me? I wasn't ready for this. My dear friend, Cathy, was standing close by and could sense how uncomfortable I was with the phone call. She leaned in, gently took the phone from my trembling hand, and said, "I'll handle this call." And she did. For several years, Cathy remained the primary contact and liaison between the agency and me. Cathy received updated information and paperwork and passed it on to me as needed. Paul's tissue, bone, and skin helped forty-five individuals, and Paul's cornea allowed someone to see.

I learned later of several selfless acts of kindness done to spare me additional pain and trauma. My friend Monica went upstairs to our master bedroom and saw traces of blood on our comforter cover. She didn't know whose blood or why the blood was there, but she feared I would see it. So, Monica removed the duvet cover from the bed and tossed it in the washing machine. It turns out that it wasn't Paul's blood. It was our yellow Labrador's blood. Our dog would sometimes lick his paws, and they would bleed. I appreciated Monica's concern and what she did to keep me from possible and unnecessary pain.

Paul's best friend and Monica's husband, Marc (a.k.a. Hawk or D.H.), and one of my brothers-in-law cleaned up the patio area in the backyard. They moved the chair where Paul sat to the side of the house, out of my view, and started scrubbing and cleaning the blood from the patio floor. No one asked them to do it. They just did it. I have often thought about how difficult that was for both men. I've also wondered if they were frustrated and cussing at Paul as they cleaned, or were they silently scrubbing in disbelief that Paul was gone and how much they already missed him?

Several people, including my children, asked me to come home with them that night instead of staying in the house. I didn't want to leave the house, and I can't explain why. Maybe I knew if I did, I might never want to return. There would be only a handful of nights I wanted to stay in that house after August 13. Overnight my dream home became a prison of haunting memories. Every time I turned onto our street, it reminded me of the day I came home and found Paul. I avoided arriving home between 5:00 pm and 5:20 pm at all costs. Every room in the house, every piece of furniture, every piece of art or framed photograph hanging on the walls reminded me of Paul and the life we shared. Each morning as I came downstairs for coffee, I glanced at the sliding glass door leading to the backyard patio where I saw Paul's foot on August 13. The last image I had of Paul haunted me daily.

Amid the indescribable pain that night, there is a beautiful moment I will never forget. When I finally wanted to lie down and attempt some semblance of sleep, several of my girlfriends followed me upstairs and fell into bed with me, holding me as I cried. Rachel Naomi Remen, the author of *Kitchen Table Wisdom*, once said, "The most basic and powerful way to connect to another person is to listen, just listen. Perhaps the most important thing we ever give each other is our attention. A loving silence often has far more power to heal and to connect than the most well-intentioned words." [4]

These women are lovingly known as the Bunco Babes. We met in 1993 when most of us moved into a new neighborhood on the same street (named White Oaks, mentioned in a previous chapter). Attempting to get to know each other, we started playing a dice game called Bunco on the second Thursday of each month. For the most part, we were all in the same life stage, around the same age, raising young children or just starting families.

On those Thursdays once a month, we played Bunco only for the first few years. We realized those precious hours together sharing a meal, drinking a glass (or two) of wine, and talking was what we wanted and needed the most. Monthly Bunco evenings were where we shared our joys and challenges, learned from one another, cried with each other, and laughed so hard we peed our pants. Barb, Sheree, Christal, Kerstin, Kat, Rosie, Tracy, Cathy, Debbie, Donna, and Linda are the real deal. These are the kind of women philosophers and authors throughout time have applauded in their writing. Separately and collectively, each of these women is authentic, available, trusting, loving, forgiving, caring, funny, independent, remarkable, and extraordinary. I am blessed to call them my friends.

As we lay huddled together in that king-size bed, we knew there was an unrecognizable and unfamiliar journey ahead for all of us. We had no playbook to follow or map to help us navigate the mountains and valleys forward, but we had each other and the unwavering belief that we could and would get through this together.

As the minutes and hours ticked slowly away from ground zero, the emotional shock which kept me insulated began to dissipate. I got a glimpse of what was left of my life as I had known it. Nothing. Around 5:00 a.m. the following day, I slipped out the front door into my courtyard with coffee in one hand and a journal in the other. In the silence and stillness of the dawn, my thoughts vacillated between, "This can't be real…he can't be gone. I don't know how to live without him," and "I can do this. I don't know how, but I have to do this!" I wrote my first entry in a journal that morning:

8/14/14 - I don't know where to start. I love you, Mr. G, and always will. Jesus, please take the wheel.[5]

Seventeen words of sweet surrender. Thirty-nine years, three months, and nineteen days with Paul were over.

It wasn't long before the house was filled again with family and friends. They came to serve. They came to grieve and lean on each other. This amazing community of family and friends selflessly put their lives on hold to help me through my darkest hours. They circled the wagons, keeping a watchful eye on me, knowing that my own life could be hanging in the balance. There was no task too big or small for my friends and neighbors. Kathy made floral arrangements for the memorial service, neighbors delivered extra chairs and tables to my home, and Donna and Meredith designed and printed the memorial programs. Friends coordinated food for the reception following the memorial, organized meal deliveries to my house, and made sure we never ran out of water, sodas, and coffee at all hours of the day and night. Linda, an original Bunco Babe, now living in Texas, flew in and quickly took control of the kitchen. She coordinated the serving of meals, prepared side dishes if needed, cleaned up, and kept snacks available at all times. Friends helped set up at the memorial service, collected all the flowers at the end of the service, and brought them to my home. They worked on a reserved seating chart, so the family knew where to sit. Cathy, our Bunco Babe with a degree in journalism, used her skills to write Paul's obituary, and she oversaw creating a beautiful video shown at the memorial. Making the final arrangements at the mortuary, picking out a few songs and photos for the video, and selecting who would speak at the memorial service were my only tasks.

With only the clothes on her back and purse in hand, my cousin Diane arrived late in the afternoon. She was on vacation with her daughter and grandkids in Florida when she got the call. She looked at her daughter and said, "Turn the car around and head to the airport. Paul died, and I have to get to Marci." Diane then called her husband, Dennis, who was working in Texas, and said, "I'm driving to the airport in Orlando. Get online and buy me a ticket on whatever airline can get me to California the fastest. I'm leaving my luggage in Florida, so pack me a bag, pack yourself a bag, and meet me at Marci's as soon as you can."

Diane and I grew up together in Texas. Diane was three years old, and I was five years old when our newly divorced mothers, cousins by marriage, moved into a small, three-bedroom home in Odessa, Texas. For two years, Diane and I shared a bedroom, and although we were cousins, we became as close as sisters. Our mothers remarried in March 1964, but we remained inseparable. When my family moved to California, Diane would visit me for weeks at a time each summer. She loved California.

Decades have passed, and I am still living in California and Diane in Texas except for eight years when she and her husband Dennis lived as ex-pats on the beautiful Caribbean island of Anguilla. We would call each other after weeks or months of not talking and pick up the conversation as though we spoke the day before. When I hear Diane's voice on the other end of the phone, I can tell in an instant if something is wrong. And vice versa. We are both fiercely protective of each other and would drop everything to get to the other if needed. When I hurt, she hurts. And she's mad as hell when I hurt. And vice versa. She's my person.

When Diane arrived, she went into action. Diane had been a legal assistant for years and was heavily involved in the Texas legal assistant's organization at the state level. She worked for top litigators and managing partners of highly respected law firms in Texas. Diane is an organized, get-things-done kind of woman. I have never known anyone that makes more "to do" lists than Diane. If a task is on Diane's list, it gets done. Friends and family quickly gave her a nickname: The Sheriff.

Diane became the contact person for questions, suggestions, and a timeline of events. Before Diane arrived, the Bunco Babes had kept a detailed record of incoming calls, meals delivered, and questions asked in the same journal I made the entry in the early morning hours. Diane continued using the same journal for notes, lists of to-dos, and other relevant information. It was genius to have all the information in one location. I still have the journal and look through it from time to time. I am still in awe of how much support I received in those first days and weeks.

Diane never took her eyes off me. She never left me alone for too long and would check on me during the night to see if I was sleeping or at least resting. When it was time to make the first trip to the mortuary to make final arrangements, Diane went with me. She meticulously took notes and asked questions I didn't think to ask or want to ask. She held my hand as I picked out Paul's urn and as I chose the keychains and necklace to engrave with Paul's fingerprint for my sons and daughter.

While Diane and I were at the mortuary, Meredith, the oldest daughter of my sweet friend Donna, purchased new patio chairs for my backyard patio. Instinctively she knew the old furniture would trigger bad memories, so it had to go. Meredith and my daughter-in-law, Kelley, picked up the chairs, delivered them to my house, and redecorated my patio. Such a thoughtful way to help. I still have those Pottery Barn patio chairs. Every time I sit in them, I'm comforted.

Diane delivered Paul's clothes to the mortuary in case my children or I wanted a last private viewing. I managed to stop my adult children from seeing their dad the day he died. I wanted them to remember their dad alive. But they were adults, and I knew I needed to offer them an opportunity to see him. Only one of my children insisted on seeing their dad, a decision soon regretted. The day before Paul's memorial service, Diane picked up Paul's ashes and brought them home.

The mortuary representative who helped us was kind and very sensitive to my loss. She told us about a friend of hers who died by suicide a month prior. Her friend spent time with her months earlier planning and paying for his funeral arrangements under the pretense of taking care of details so the family would not need to in the event of his death years later. The mortuary representative felt betrayed when her friend died by suicide shortly after making his arrangements. So, because of her own experience, she told me she would go the extra mile for me and do her best to honor any requests I had. And she did. Our first meeting with her was on Friday, August 15, and on Monday, August 18, fifteen copies of Paul's death certificate were ready to be picked up at the mortuary. Getting the death certificates was a miracle. Obtaining a death certificate typically takes two to three weeks at the earliest. I had them in four days.

Paul's memorial service was held one week later on what would have been his fifty-ninth birthday. It was standing room only. I was overwhelmed when I walked into the service with my kids and saw many people celebrating Paul's life. Families we knew from the twelve years we participated in our local baseball Little League, neighbors, church members, ex-employees, customers, vendors, college friends, and even representatives from our largest business competitor attended the memorial service. Pastor Kenny delivered a powerful message of hope, and my brother, Mark, gave a funny, heartfelt eulogy describing Paul and the impact he had on so many. It was a beautiful service, and all I did was show up. From start to finish, our friends orchestrated all the details.

A reception followed the service. Kris, Cory, Dani, and I stood in a receiving line for over two hours, receiving hugs, shaking hands, and thanking people for attending. Another beautiful tribute to Paul. Diane stood behind me, handing me cups of water every so often. After two hours, my friends insisted I sit down and try to eat. I sat for a few minutes and then got up and moved from table to table, thanking people once again for their attendance at Paul's service. I was physically exhausted when the reception was over but filled with love.

As I mentioned earlier, having Paul's death certificate was critical. Paul and I owned a vacation home in Lake Havasu, Arizona, for thirteen years. At the time of Paul's death, we were in the process of selling the vacation home and expected to sign escrow papers on Friday, August 22, in Lake Havasu. We included most of the furniture in the house's sale, but I needed to retrieve our personal belongings and a couple of furniture pieces.

Before Paul died, we signed and notarized escrow papers and FedExed them to Arizona's escrow agent. One document requiring our signatures had fallen off Paul's desk on the floor in his office, and he didn't see it. The escrow agent called me the day before Paul's memorial and alerted me to the missing paperwork. I explained Paul died and asked what she needed to complete the escrow process. The escrow agent was a widow herself and told me to go ahead and travel to Lake Havasu as planned and bring a copy of the death certificate with me.

The day following the memorial service, my kids, Diane, and I packed up and drove five hours to Lake Havasu, Arizona. I brought Paul's death certificate with me, and the escrow agent allowed me to sign the last document on Paul's behalf. If she had not helped me, the house would have fallen out of escrow, and I would be on my own to sell it.

Lake Havasu represented a lifetime of family memories. So many fun days beginning with launching boats in the early morning hours followed by hours of wakeboarding, long boat rides, wet yellow labs fetching sticks in the water, and friends and family floating on rafts for hours in private coves. Most days, we stayed out on the lake until just before dusk unless monsoonal thunderstorms rolled in. Paul loved the lake, especially surrounded by his family.

While in Havasu, we had a private memorial service for Paul. On Saturday morning, twelve of us headed out on Lake Havasu aboard Kris's boat. We found a perfect cove, peaceful and isolated, and anchored the boat. With seventies music playing in the background, we laid flowers on the beach, waded into the water, and silently said our final goodbyes. The details of exactly where we memorialized Paul are private and known only to the family, but somewhere on Lake Havasu is a cove named Glidden Cove. There were lots of tears and lots of smiles and laughter aboard the boat as we made our way back to the dock. Everyone knew Paul loved this lake, and he would be happy knowing we were there. I'm so thankful people helped make that day so special. Still numb from Paul's death, I don't know if I could have walked away from thirteen years of family memories otherwise.

On the well-known Holmes & Rahe Stress Scale, a spouse's death is number 1 and considered one of life's most devastating events. You never get over it. Never. You can get through it and past it, but you never get over it. Losing the love of your life, partner, best friend, lover, co-parent, peer, date, travel partner, bunker buddy, the one you dreamed with and thought you would grow old with, the one who knew you best, the good, the bad and the ugly.

The emotional fallout is impossible to describe to someone who has never experienced this loss. I felt like I was free-falling into an abyss of unwanted and unknown despair. Sadness, loneliness, and disbelief were overwhelming. My instinctive "fight or flight" response was to supernaturally step back in time and do something, say something, anything, to change this outcome. The physical pain can leave you short of breath, curled up in a fetal position, longing for their touch. A memory, a song, a photo, a smell, a piece of furniture, a sound, or even a comment can trigger unexpected and uncontrollable emotions from sadness to anger.

Every day was stressful. Every decision I made or the task I needed to accomplish was hard and reminded me Paul was gone, and I was alone. But I couldn't give Grief my undivided attention. My kids were grieving! They've lost one parent; they can't lose another one. So, I did what I felt I had to do. I kept my Grief private as much as I could and jumped into full-no-holds-barred Mom mode. I knew I couldn't fix it, but I was determined to do anything and everything to help them.

My journal entry — 9/10/2014: My life changed forever! You left me alone. You left me to deal with and suffer through the indescribable Grief of Kris, Cory, and Dani. Their pain is like a sharp dagger piercing my heart, and I can't make it go away. They miss you so much, and their sense of security is lost! You were their safety net. They have to learn to face the world without you. And so do I. I've always called you an A**hole (joking most of the time), but I want to scream "A**HOLE" at the top of my lungs right now!!![6]

CHAPTER 6
Grief Moves In

"Grief sucks!" [1]
Said Everyone Ever

C.S. Lewis observed, "Part of every misery is, so to speak, the misery's shadow or reflection; the fact that you don't merely suffer but have to keep on thinking about the fact that you suffer. I not only live each endless day in Grief but live each day thinking about living each day in Grief." [2] A beautiful and well-written description of living with Grief!

It would be great if you could Google "how to do Grief well" and some awesome YouTube video appears with a day-to-day, week-to-week, month-to-month tutorial to follow. The tutorial would give you examples of what to expect on this journey, triggers that can cause so much pain, family and friends who won't know what to say or do. How to deal with emotions you will feel simultaneously—sadness and joy, hope and despair, loneliness, freedom, anger, and love. ***Most everyone will experience Grief at some time in their life, so why are we so underprepared for the inevitable?***

Grief is a personal and unique journey. No two are the same, making the process even more lonely and isolating. There is no right or wrong way to grieve; how you process Grief is not subject to anyone's opinion but your own. It's your call and yours alone. There is no time limit on Grief. There is no magical, imaginary date separating what you can or can't do by a predetermined date. In general, it's a good idea not to make major decisions after the death of a spouse, like selling a home, quitting a job, moving, or giving away your loved one's belongings. But you can and will have to make some decisions, like funeral arrangements, how to inform family and friends about the death, filling out the death certificate, etc. Remember, you have lost a loved one, not your integrity or ability to make correct decisions or complete required tasks.

You also can't measure the pain of losing someone you love. You can't point to the sixth face on the Wong-Baker Pain Rating Scale (worst pain ever) and say, "That's it!" Grief is different for *everyone*. My Grief was not more harrowing, nor more painful, nor more devastating; it was just different. My Grief over the loss of a husband was unlike the pain my children felt losing their dad—not worse or more painful, just slightly different. The pain my two daughters-in-laws and son-in-law felt when Paul died was no less challenging or less sad or less devastating. It's just different. The Grief our extended family and friends felt was also different. And Grief never goes away. It's part of you, for better or for worse.

Grief will, and does, show up—suddenly, unexpectedly—after months or years. And you're on your own to navigate as best you can in dark uncharted waters. I don't think anyone is ever really prepared for the onslaught of emotions following a loved one's death. How can you be? The mere thought of living without them is uncomfortable and unbearable.

For me, not being able to describe how I feel to family and friends adequately is frustrating. Some days I can push Grief below the surface and keep moving forward. Other days I'm swallowed up by pain and the feeling that it will never end. The daily balancing act I play in my mind is challenging for me to understand, much less try to explain. When someone asks me how I'm doing, it's easier to say, "I'm OK."

Megan Devine, psychotherapist, grief advocate, and author of *It's OK That You're Not OK,* offers her unique perspective and insight on Grief after losing her partner in 2009. To students in her Writing Your Grief classes, she suggests that writing about your Grief can help. I was fascinated by the following writing prompt she gave her students: "If you were writing fiction, you'd want to know the voice of your main character. You'd want to know the way they walk, the kinds of food they eat, how they comb their hair. They would need to be *real.* In a way, your Grief is a character; it has a rhythm and a voice. It is particular to you. If we're going to be working with Grief, let's find out who it is. The creative tool is called *personification.* What we're doing is giving Grief itself a voice. When it has a voice, it can tell us things. Let's think of this exercise as inviting your Grief to introduce himself or herself to you."[3]

I would not have been able to do this writing exercise one or two or even three years out, from Paul's death, but I know Grief now, and I know my Grief has a voice. Here is how I met Grief.

Grief must have arrived while I was still being sheltered in shock in those first hours after discovering Paul's lifeless body. She did her reconnaissance, assessed the situation, took note of the other cast members, and made a list of the emotional tools she would need for the job when she moved in with me. Permanently.

The first time I remember feeling her presence was later that evening, or in the early morning hours of August 14, the first time I doubled over in pain and realized this was real. She followed me around like a silent stalker. Everywhere I turned, she was there. She keeps her eyes on me, always ready to abruptly intervene in a conversation, a thought, or a mood. I don't want her here. I don't like her. And I am annoyed that she looks just like me. She's my twin: same blue eyes, same gray roots peeping out from under the brown hair, the same manner of clothing, same voice. And she knows something I don't know.

At first, I scream at her, "Who the hell are you? You don't belong here! I can't catch my breath when you are near me. Go away. Please, just go away!"

She turns toward me and quietly says, "My name is Grief, and I'm here because you loved Paul. I'm the consequence of losing someone you love. I'm Pandora's box of emotions that no one talks about until they have no choice. It's impossible for me to leave because you loved him."

This unwelcome guest then plops herself down on my couch and continues, "I suppose you can ignore me for a while. Pretend you're OK. Put a smile on your face and go about business as usual. You're strong; that's what everyone says about you. You could try and numb me away with medications and alcohol. But that's not you, never has been, although I would understand if you did. After all, your husband just shot himself in the head on your back porch, and you found him! It may work for a while, but I will still be here when that doesn't work anymore. By the way, none of the choices will be good for you. None of them. They will just lead to more pain."

By now, I am exhausted, in excruciating emotional pain, mad as hell, and done with this houseguest. I scream, "Really? More pain? I'm living with the most pain I have ever felt in my life! Missing him hurts so bad. He promised me he was OK, and I believed him. I can't watch my children's pain; it's unbearable. I can't fix it. I can't explain it. I can't make it go away. I can't protect him; everyone knows he killed himself. I have to live with this nightmare for the rest of my life. I didn't ask for this pain. It wasn't my choice; it would have never been my choice! His death is not my fault!"

Usually, an unpleasant display of gut-wrenching pain and anger would clear the room. I expected Grief to pick herself up off the couch with her tail between her legs and say, "You're right, Marci. You don't deserve this pain and sorrow, and neither do your children or your family or friends. I'm so sorry for showing up unannounced and uninvited. Of course, this is just a bad nightmare, and tomorrow you will wake up, and I will be gone."

No such luck. Instead, Grief slowly stood up, approached me with the resolve of a Five Star General in the middle of battle, and says, "This is my game, and you will play by my rules. You can scream, cry, pout, ignore me, and curse at me all you want, but I am not leaving. Not now. Not ever. I'm your new roommate, constant companion, stalker, and bodyguard. I will be with you 24/7, every day for the rest of your life. I am the ONLY one who knows what you are feeling. I'm your Grief, and I'm unique to you. I'm not here to just help you survive. I am here to show you how to live again. I know you don't believe that now, but you will someday."

Did I hear Grief, right? Forever? 24/7? NO! NO! NO!

"Yes, you heard me right; this is forever, but you have a choice. You can stay mired in the overwhelming sadness and plod along each day, never knowing what lies ahead, or you can let me lead you. I'm not going to sugarcoat this journey. It sucks. It's hard and miserable and long and scary, and very, very lonely. You must commit to doing the work necessary to accept me, explore me, understand me, and ultimately learn from me so you can move past me to a new, good, joyful, and love-filled life. Allowing me to teach you is your choice. Remember, I am here only because you loved someone."

And like a bad habit, Grief was there every morning when I woke up, every night when I went to bed and, every moment in-between. She followed me everywhere and could always withstand any emotion I threw at her. Oddly enough, she was a safe place to fall. She could quietly sit while I cried or encourage me to get my anger out when I would throw a pity party. She understood the opposing emotions I could feel simultaneously, like anger and acceptance, hopelessness and hope, sorrow and joy. And she witnessed every private moment along my journey that I was not ready to reveal or admit to anyone, including anger.

I have been asked several times, "Aren't you angry?" Angry? You bet I'm angry. But I have kept my anger private for the most part. My kids have heard my anger, especially my sons. Working together every day with a steep learning curve was not easy. I didn't want the responsibility of our family business. I didn't want to walk into the same office building that I was in the very last time I saw Paul alive. I wanted to fall into bed for days and cry. My life had imploded, and the thought of getting up every day, going to the office, and making critical decisions was complex. Most books on Grief recommend not making BIG decisions early. I didn't have that luxury. Every day, my sons and I had to make business decisions that affected our sustainability and every employee we had—all big and important decisions.

Looking back, I think the first sign that I was angry might have been days after Paul died. I told my cousin Diane I was having a hard time walking into my closet because Paul's clothes were there. I didn't want to see them or touch them. I needed his clothes out of the closet immediately. I pretended to need a safe sanctuary in the house. A place I could escape to if I became overwhelmed. The truth is I didn't want to see Paul's clothes because I was so angry at him for what he had just done. I was thinking, "If he thought he could just check out on me after all these years with no warning, no good-bye, no note or explanation, then his clothes didn't deserve to be in my bedroom any longer."

Another "mad as hell" episode was shortly after Paul's memorial service. I was alone in the house, and I started yelling at Paul for leaving me. I yelled and screamed and cussed at Paul for over an hour. "Why did you leave me? Did you not love me? Was I not worth staying alive for? I loved you with everything I had, and you let me find you? Why did you leave me with that image? You left everyone with questions! You left me to answer all those questions! How could you do this to our kids? They're devastated! They have put you on a pedestal so high that no one can equal you, not even me! Sometimes I feel like they don't see me. They only see you! Newsflash: I'm the one still here. I didn't leave without saying good-bye. I haven't checked out on them. You did it!" Along with the verbal assault aimed at Paul, I threw a few things around the house just to prove my point.

That would not be my last angry episode. Expressing my anger, albeit in private, was a good release, but it didn't move me forward on my journey. I misdirected my rage. I should have been angry at the illness that robbed Paul of his life. Not at how he died. If Paul had cancer and ultimately lost his battle when his lungs filled with pneumonia, I would be angry at cancer and not pneumonia.

Grief witnessed all my misdirected tantrums, sitting quietly in a room as I raged. Grief understood I wasn't ready to learn from her until I was tired of her sting and wretched smell. So, Grief played hardball with me. She interjected into conversations with friends. She clouded my thoughts, making it difficult to express what I was trying to say. She delighted in whispering in my ear during a romantic scene in a movie, "See what you're missing?" I constantly battled with Grief. I thought I could outrun her and certainly outsmart her. After all, I'm a strong and resilient woman. But I was wrong. Grief could produce an avalanche of emotions by unleashing her secret weapons. Some people call them triggers or landmines. I call them sinkholes because I didn't see them coming until I felt the ground below me collapsing and tears welling in my eyes.

MY SINKHOLES

Filling out forms - Shortly after Paul's death, I had my annual appointment for my mammogram. I arrived on time, checked in, and received an iPad to update my contact information and medical history. A few questions in, I came to the boxes you check to provide your status: Single - Married

- Divorced - Widowed. The tears started welling up as I checked the box labeled widow for the first time, and all I could think was *I'm widowed*. Oh, God, I'm widowed.

Listing emergency contacts - I didn't want to pick someone else. I want my husband to be the first called. My husband is the only one who knows everything about me—what medical care I would like or refuse, my social security number, my blood type, what medicines I might be taking, and on and on. More importantly, it would be my husband who could hold my hand and make me feel as though everything would be all right. My husband was always my safe place to fall.

Weddings - I think it's fair to say that most wedding guests get sentimental during a wedding ceremony. They are holding their partner's hand and thinking about their special day. The music, the vows, the entire atmosphere is all about love and the future. Attending a wedding as a widow was very hard. I kept thinking about the words "until death do us part" and how that feels.

Holidays - For me, Christmas, Thanksgiving, and Easter were not generally hard. On those days, family and friends enveloped me in love and kept me occupied and focused on all the beautiful festivities of the day. The days leading up to the significant holidays were a different story. The decorations, the china, the traditions were OURS, not just mine. One of the most challenging moments for me was opening the box of Christmas stockings. Right on top was his stocking. He loved the Christmas stocking I made for him. Sitting on the garage floor and crying, I kept thinking, What do I do with this? Do I hang it up in memoriam? Will that make the family uncomfortable, or will it be comforting? If I don't hang it up, what does that mean? Sitting on the floor of the garage, in the middle of a weekend day, holding a Christmas stocking and crying.

<u>Seeing other couples</u> - Sometimes, just seeing other couples brings on a painful and solemn conversation in my mind. I want back what I lost. I miss my husband desperately and the way our bodies moved together. I miss the mundane, ordinary trips to Home Depot together for an item on his honey-do list. I miss the playful and sexual tension between us when we are getting ready for a date night. I miss taking turns picking the movie we will see together. And I miss holding his hand. I miss everything about us!

<u>The grocery store</u> - Years ago, when my kids were young, going to the grocery store alone was a treat—one precious hour of quiet time. No kids were hanging off the shopping cart or asking for this or that—only me pushing a shopping cart down one aisle and up the next at my pace. Now, the grocery store is one giant sinkhole waiting to happen. I grab a smaller cart now because I don't need a larger grocery cart. Focusing on all the items I need has morphed into focusing on all the things I no longer need: his favorite bread or favorite ice cream or favorite shaving cream. I have sat in the grocery store parking lot many times crying. A few times, I've driven back home and avoided it altogether because Grief can stop you in your tracks anytime, anywhere, leaving your thoughts frozen in memory.

<u>Greeting cards</u> - I enjoy sending greeting cards to my family and friends for the most significant holidays throughout the year. As crazy as it sounds, I can spend quite a bit of time standing in the grocery store's card section or local car wash looking for the right cards. Sometimes, I buy cards of all kinds, so I have them if I need them, like get-well cards, encouragement cards, and birthday cards. Excluding annual Christmas cards, Halloween cards are my all-time favorite cards to send—crazy, funny, spooky, and wildly colorful Halloween cards.

And Halloween cards pop up mid-summer when you least expect them—4th of July decorations pushed to the clearance aisle to make room for pumpkins, candy, costumes, and the rich, cozy colors and smells of fall. I won't be surprised if Independence Day gets skipped altogether; ghosts and goblins appear after the cute little chicks and furry bunnies, much like Thanksgiving between Halloween and Christmas. So, on a hot summer day in shorts and flip-flops, I pop into my local grocery store for a few items, stroll past the greeting card section, and run head-on into Grief.

I saw a Halloween card with two smiling ghosts holding hands and smiling with the words "you & me" juxtaposed in black. It was a sweet card but all too familiar to me. One year earlier, I bought the same card for my husband. In the grocery store, standing in front of a card rack staring at Halloween cards, my husband's death was brand new—again. I felt my heart racing, tears welling in my eyes, and I couldn't stop the playback of the night he died. Grief appears in the least likely places at unexpected times. Another example of the many steps taken backward following one complex and brave step forward.

Simple "How are you" - Questions can be a catch-22. It's hard to determine if the question warrants a truthful answer or if the question is simply a polite greeting. Was I expected to say, "I'm fine," and move on, or was it an invitation to share the truth of my reality? Either way, I was often in a no-win situation. Running into acquaintances I hadn't seen since his death could open a floodgate of emotions. Sometimes the conversation would start with, "Oh Marci, I heard what happened! How are you?" Although it was a sincere question, I knew it meant telling the story repeatedly, which meant hearing more questions. So, I would say, "I'm fine," and try to steer the conversation in a different direction.

I mentioned this in a therapy session, and my therapist said, "It's OK to tell the truth, Marci. You don't have to tell people you're fine when you're not." Easier said than done. Soon after that therapy session, I was out to dinner with friends, and someone asked me how I was. I said, "My life sucks. How are you?" Maybe it was my delivery because my comment wasn't well-received. Perhaps I should have said, "I feel devastated," or "I'm doing the best I can under unimaginable circumstances" instead of "my life sucks." It's hard to discern between sincerity and foolish small talk. Now I usually just say, "I'm fine. Thank you," and move on.

Unexpected reminders - can drop you to your knees. They are different for everyone, and they can be anything from a photograph to a song to an article of clothing and everything in-between. Months after my husband's death, I dropped my phone on the floor next to our bed. As I reached down to pick it up, I noticed a small orange item under the bed. I reached under the bed to grab it, and once I saw what it was, I sat down and starting crying. It was the orange zip tie that I had cut off the bag containing his personal effects from the coroner's office. In an instant, that little orange zip tie sent me back to those first few hours after he was gone. The intense pain from losing him was forefront in my mind like it just happened.

Social media was a mixed bag. It could be valuable and helpful or harmful and hurtful. How my husband died was exposed and left open for public comments and speculations. I wanted to protect him and his reputation as long as I could. Individuals simply ignored his privacy, my privacy, and the family's privacy. The stigma surrounding suicide is real, and it is painful for grieving family and friends. I had no control over what anyone posted and sometimes couldn't discern the intent of a post.

Weekends are painful. Before my husband's death, weekends were for date nights, dinners with friends, catching a movie, binge-watching a Netflix series together, napping together on a rainy Sunday afternoon, or heading out of town for a weekend adventure. Now the weekend involves seventy-two long hours of solitude. Occasionally, I have plans with a friend, but not usually. For years I looked forward to Friday and the beginning of a fun weekend. Now I look forward to Mondays because it means the weekend is over.

Going to bed at night tops my list of sinkholes. I still have trouble describing the overwhelming sadness and loneliness that crawls into bed with me every night. I couldn't sleep beneath the covers for over two months after my husband's death. My beautiful king-size bed was the most powerful reminder that the man I loved and the life I cherished were gone. Forever. Lysa Terkeurst, the author of *It's Not Supposed to Be This Way*, offers this visual: *"But the sun still goes down tonight. The darkness envelopes my quiet home. And my husband won't be there to whisper, 'You're not alone. At least we have each other, and we'll get through this together.'"*

PHYSICAL CHANGES OF GRIEF

Grief physically hurts. Mystery pains like sore muscles, aching joints, headaches, memory loss, insomnia, weight changes, and a rapid heartbeat are all common physical effects of Grief. Stress can affect your body, and as mentioned earlier, the loss of a spouse is Number 1 on the stress scale.

Healthy sleep patterns are disrupted, limiting restorative sleep. Some people sleep all the time. Others like myself don't sleep enough. For most of my life, including when I was pregnant, I could sleep like a baby—rarely waking up in the middle of the night. Now, not so much. Most of the time, I don't go to bed until midnight and wake up at least once a night. And when I do wake up in the middle of the night, it's not because I need to go to the bathroom. I wake up, reaching for my husband, who isn't there. Sometimes I'm startled when I wake up because I think I see him lying next to me, and I'm not sure if I'm dreaming or waking from a bad nightmare.

Grief affects your diet. Either you overeat or rarely eat. Either way, it's not healthy. An unhealthy diet can lead to digestion issues, weight changes, heartburn, and more. For me, eating is tricky, and cooking is almost impossible. When the kids left for college, it was challenging to learn to cook for two after so many years. Cooking for one was nothing more than another reminder that the life I loved was gone.

If you have ever seen the 1991 film *Thelma and Louise*, you might remember the scene when the detective, played by Harvey Keitel, is looking around Louise's apartment for clues while Thelma and Louise were on the run. The camera pans through the apartment and slowly zooms in on the one glass next to the kitchen sink. Most days, that's what my kitchen resembles. Many times, I stand in the kitchen and think about what a waste of space. The plates, glasses, and silverware never rotate through a cycle. I never use the bottom ten out of twelve dinner plates. I don't use any drinking glasses past the first row on the shelf, and twenty-two out of twenty-four forks and knives sit silently in the silverware drawer unless it was a major holiday or a family get-together for someone's birthday. I turn on the dishwasher most of the time when it's only one-quarter full to avoid a musty smell.

Grief is exhausting. Simple mundane tasks can take forever to complete. It's sometimes hard to remember what I accomplished or didn't. Days and nights roll into each other without distinction. Phone calls, texts, and emails are left unanswered. It was challenging to stay focused and engaged in simple conversations. Grief drains your energy and disrupts your ability to focus. When I talked to my friend, a widower, he said there were days when he left his office at lunch to take a nap.

Your social calendar changes. It's hard to be with someone who's grieving and in pain. You don't know what to say, and you fear to say the wrong thing. That's legitimate and understandable. For couples, I think it's incredibly challenging to be around a grieving widow or widower. Unless husband and wife fall asleep one night hand in hand and wakes up in the loving arms of God together, the widow or widower represents the future for the couple. How far off in the future is never known. Mortality is a difficult concept to embrace. And let's face it, no one wants to be in my shoes. No one!

So, for the most part, your social calendar frees up. It's not that your coupled friends don't love you. It's just awkward. Several couples invite me to dinner or a movie occasionally, and I am so grateful. Because for one evening, I feel as close to normal as I can get because Grief leaves me alone.

When Grief moves in, everything changes.

CHAPTER 7

Liminality

"She understood that the hardest times in life to go through were when you were transitioning from one version of yourself to another." [1]
—Sarah Addison Allen

Sometimes I felt like I was in between a rock and a hard place. My past life was over, sealed shut with an impermeable boulder: the hard place—my future—hidden behind the horizon. I existed in the in-between, not aware of the significance of liminality until I benefited from hindsight. That is when I saw how much I had learned about myself.

Grief was not my only new roommate. Two weeks after Paul's death, my daughter Dani, her new fiancé Mike, and Mandy moved into my home so I wouldn't be alone. Mandy was like another daughter to Paul and me. She and Dani met when they were five years old in a dance class in our neighborhood and had been best friends ever since. I went from being an empty nester with Paul dreaming about our future retirement to a widow with a house full of roommates and working full-time. Everything in my life had changed.

It was good to have activity back in the house, and it made being in the place bearable most days. But having roommates could also be a double-edged sword. My mood and things I would say were noticed, analyzed, and often shared with friends and family. I understood watchful eyes were well-meaning and came from a place of concern, but sometimes I masked my true feelings to maintain some privacy. Grief was the only new roommate I couldn't fool; she knew exactly how I was doing at all times. Grief would whisper in my ear, "Marci, you can't ignore me. I'm here, and I will always be here."

THE BUSINESS

I couldn't fall into bed and cry for days and weeks. We had a family business to run. At least, we hoped we did. Our company was Paul's dream, and he was the face of the business for the past twenty-five years. Both our sons, Kris and Cory, worked for the family business. Kris was our only other salesman, and Cory was learning the ins and outs of our manufacturing facility in Texas and our logistics operation in Mexico. But Paul had been a typical entrepreneur and continued to micromanage any responsibilities he relinquished to our sons, never allowing them to succeed or fail on their own. Paul was always ready and willing to throw out a safety net if needed.

My journal entry - 11/5/2014: I don't want to do this! I can't do this! I want to wake up from this nightmare and be your wife again. I can't fill your shoes. No one can. What if I fail? What if I mess everything up? What if I destroy everything you worked so hard to build? [2]

So here we were, given the reins to our family business with no warning, no preparation, while in the grip of Grief, and without the one key person to ask who knew everything about the company. It would require each of us to work harder and smarter than ever before and trust that all of us would do our best as we stepped up. Paul nurtured and maintained relationships with nationally branded clients and vendors for decades. He could predict what the P & L would say each month, usually within $1000. He built a successful business, was well respected in the industry, leaving a legacy of integrity and commitment to excellence, and did whatever it took to get the job done. All the pressure and stress of running a business Paul had known and felt for twenty-five years was now ours. These were very BIG shoes to fill.

In the beginning, our business attorney advised us not to disclose the actual cause of Paul's death to our clients, vendors, employees, and other business associates. He felt it would be in the business's best interest to simply say Paul had suddenly passed due to a blood clot. Not disclosing the truth was an extra burden we carried for several years. The vast majority of our clients and vendors remained loyal and allowed us to remain a viable and essential packaging supplier. I am forever grateful to some key vendors who came alongside my sons as mentors to answer questions and talk through business strategies. I am also incredibly thankful for the executive team of one of our nationally branded clients who offered to send us a consulting firm they partnered with to help us if needed.

The pressure associated with running the company wasn't easy. The truth is, most of the time, I hated it! Most of the time, I was scared. And most of the time, I was angry at Paul for putting me in this position. I felt as though the pressure Paul felt to succeed and keep our business growing was now mine. Paul was very proud that our sons wanted to work alongside him and eventually run the business themselves. But having your sons work for the family business has a downside, too. Besides the typical concerns of any family business, Paul felt responsible for our sons' families. The business decisions Paul made affected not only him and me but our kids as well. Some people might argue Kris and Cory chose to work for the family business and, therefore, the boys were responsible for their families' financial stability and not Paul's. It's a fair and valid opinion, but not one Paul chose.

In the first weeks following Paul's death, I leaned on advisors to determine if my best option was to sell our company or keep it. All of my advisors agreed that with guidance, I should keep the business. My priority was to inform our bank of Paul's passing and decide to continue personally guaranteeing the receivable line of financing. Kris and Cory notified our customers and vendors and reassured them it was business as usual. At the time, one of our nationally branded clients represented about fifty-five percent of our business. I made a point to meet with this client's executive team to reassure them we were financially viable, and our vendors were on board to continue providing products.

Our employees at our manufacturing facility in El Paso, Texas, and our logistics facility in Mexicali, Mexico, needed reassurance that the business would continue and secure their jobs. Many employees had worked for the company for over ten years, and they liked and respected Paul. As with our customers and vendors, attorneys advised us not to tell our employees the truth about how Paul died. We needed to continue business as usual as much as we could. Paul's death was challenging, in and of itself, and the truth of how Paul died would have been unnecessarily shocking.

Three or four weeks after Paul's memorial service, I flew to El Paso to speak with our employees and assure them we were still in business and their jobs were secure. It wasn't a comfortable meeting. Most employees hadn't seen me in years, and some employees had never met me. Now I'm their boss? My first decision as the new CEO was to promote a female supervisor as the new General Manager for our Texas facility. Employees didn't know Paul had been grooming her for this position but had not put the plan into action. She had been with us for over fifteen years and learned more about our company's manufacturing side than we did. But the take-away for the employees was seeing a woman promote a woman.

Our General Manager in our logistics facility in Mexico had also been with us for a very long time. When our largest client moved their manufacturing facility from California to Mexico in 2004, we became part of the NAFTA program as a maquiladora to continue as a primary packaging supplier for our client. Paul and our G.M. in Mexico were the only ones who knew all the details of our status as a maquila and a critical change in the Mexican laws beginning in January 2015. The Mexican government cracked down on companies that claimed to be maquilas but weren't, so they implemented a new certification process to weed out illegal companies. If our company was not certified by January 1, 2015, we would be responsible for the 16% VAT on all products or raw materials imported to Mexico. Our company was headed in the right direction but couldn't afford to lose money following the losses incurred from 2008 to 2010 by two customers who closed their doors owing us just under a quarter million dollars.

We had three months to prepare the new law's documentation and hire Mexican attorneys in Mexico City to advise and represent us. Also, we needed to find a company experienced with the latest software required for compliance with the new law, install the software, train employees, and offer continuing support with yearly recertification. And we needed to communicate in Spanish and English. We were late to the game, so it's no surprise we temporarily lost our certification in early 2015, causing us to pay the 16% VAT. I invested money into the business to cover the loss, hoping I was making the right decision. It was a very stressful time, and I was furious.

My journal entry – 1/14/2015: Paul, is this the kind of stress you had every day? I'm so sorry I didn't understand how stressful it was for you! I thought I did, but I didn't. You would always say that it was "good" stress. Did you lie to me? I need to talk to you. I need your advice. I need you to hold me and tell me it's all going to be okay. You left me to feel all this pain and stress by myself. You always had me cheer you on, listen and encourage you, and love you no matter what happened. Who do I have? No one. [3]

I wasn't the only one who secretly felt the responsibility of keeping our company in business. Both my sons felt the same sense of responsibility, but in different ways. Kris was now the only salesperson on board. Without sales, companies don't grow. Kris was responsible for maintaining our current customer base and for finding opportunities to acquire new customers. Cory was now in charge of overseeing our manufacturing facility in Texas, our logistics facility in Mexico, and maintaining and growing a relationship with our most extensive, nationally branded customer. Kris and Cory faced new challenges and added responsibilities while grieving the loss of their dad, their mentor, and their Number 1 hero. A mom and two sons catapulted into new roles with only two options—sink or swim.

Every day we walked back into the same building Paul walked out of on August 13. His surfboard still hangs in our office today. Whiteboards line the walls with essential details in Paul's printing. Post-It® notes stuck to his computer screen as reminders of upcoming meetings or part numbers for a customer. A grieving family working together could have been a disaster. This dynamic could have broken family relationships beyond repair and put us out of business. But it didn't! We started swimming. We learned from our mistakes, and we found ways through and around obstacles; we sought solutions to problems, asked questions, and listened to advice.

And every evening, when I came home to a house full of new roommates, Grief was waiting for me. I got good at ignoring Grief during the day at work. I was too busy trying to stay afloat. But at night, Grief was hard to ignore. For me, Grief felt like a cold fog slowly seeping into my body, clouding my heart, my soul, and my mind with unwanted loneliness. The moment I started my evening ritual of turning the lights off downstairs, checking to make sure all the doors are locked, and walking upstairs, I could feel Grief's presence. Every night as I shut the bedroom door behind me, I glanced at Paul's empty side of the bed, and the tears would fall. No words, just tears. Max Lucado describes tears as, "Those tiny drops of humanity. Those round, wet balls of fluid that tumble from your eyes creep down our cheeks and splash on the floor of our hearts. They were there that day. They are always present at such times. They should be; that's their job. They are miniature messengers, on-call twenty-four hours a day to substitute for crippled words. They drip, drop, and pour from our souls, carrying with them the deepest emotions we possess. They tumble down our faces with announcements that range from the most blissful joy to darkest despair. The principle is simple; when words are most empty, tears are most apt."[4]

THE FIRSTS

After Paul's death, I spent the first year primarily focused on our family business and our daughter's wedding. But I also spent a lot of time anticipating and planning for all the "firsts" — first Father's Day, first Christmas, the first anniversary of Paul's death, and how I could help ease Kris, Cory, and Dani's pain. Maybe that's why the second year was so much harder for me.

The first Christmas, I took the kids, their spouses, fiancé, and my grandson to Hawaii. I didn't want to be at home, and I don't think the kids did, either. We had a good time under the circumstances. Lying by the pool, drinking Mai Tais all day, and being together helped ease our pain. It had only been 135 days since Paul's death. In retrospect, I think we were all still shrouded in disbelief and merely going through the motions each day. We had no idea what the future held or the strength of Grief's grip on each of us. Maybe that was a good thing.

Father's Day. The holiday I dreaded the most. I wasn't sure what I should do, if anything. On the first Father's Day, I decided to make something special for Kris, Cory, and Dani. I used some of Paul's clothes and had quilts made for each kid out of the clothes; unique t-shirts, sweatshirts, board shorts, dress shirts, and ties Paul always wore. The kids loved the quilts and said the quilts were the best gifts I gave them. Over the years, Kris, Cory, and Dani created their traditions in honor of their dad each Father's Day. Kris seeks comfort at the lake or near a beach, participating in various water sports he enjoyed with Paul. Cory watches the U.S. Open golf tournament. Paul and Cory shared a love for playing golf and talking about golf. Dani writes a special message to her dad on a blue balloon each year and releases it.

On the first anniversary of Paul's death, we wanted to be together. So, I rented each of us a waterfront room at a beautiful hotel in Laguna Beach for the day and night. I encouraged each family member to write a letter to Paul to share if they felt led. After a fun dinner at a local pub and a few shots of courage, we gathered together in my hotel room. One family member chose to keep their letter and thoughts private, a decision we honored and respected. Sitting in silence, breathing in every heart-wrenching, honest, and poignant word, we listened as each person read their letter. Vulnerability is not easy for a lot of people. We were allowed entry into each other's private world of Grief. We offered no solutions. We passed no judgments. It reminded me of Brené Brown's quote, "If you're not in the arena also getting your ass kicked, I'm not interested in your feedback." [5] We offered no feedback. We leaned in and met them in their pain. Here are some excerpts from my letter to Paul.

August 13, 2015

Paul,

It's been 365 days since I hugged you and woke up in the morning with you next to me. It's been a very long year since I forgave you and kissed you good-bye. There is so much I want to say to you. But the most important thing is I love you, I have always loved you, and I will always love you. I miss you every day. I miss the one person in this world who knew me better than anyone. I miss being your wife. I miss your long hair and the way you smelled. I miss feeling safe. I miss your political commentary and putting your foot in your mouth. I miss loving you because I was good at that. I miss you being in love with me, not just loving me, but being in love with me.

Everything has changed. The life I knew and enjoyed doesn't exist anymore. It vanished in a split second, and there was nothing I could have done to stop it. We had a thirty-nine-and-a- half-year romance. We understood each other and loved unconditionally. Neither one of us was perfect, but we learned to compromise, accept, and move past the other's faults in our beautiful journey together. We respected each other and gave each additional space when needed. We supported each other's dreams and goals. And we never gave up on ourselves! I recently read that "Sudden loss takes you to places you never asked to visit. It takes you on unchartered, mysterious, unfamiliar journeys to the depth of our souls, where we clatter and crash about, slog through the molasses of Grief and come out the other side. Although death surely ends a life, it never ends a relationship."[6]

And we were blessed with three unique and remarkable children. You were always so very proud of each of them, and I know you still are. You were an awesome dad and would do anything for them. So many dads are absent in their children's lives, but not you. You were there for everything: baseball games, football games, wrestling matches, soccer games on fields near and far, Indian guides, award ceremonies, elementary school plays, middle school music presentations, and high school dances. Sending each kid off to college and all those college moves from dorms to home to apartments to sorority and fraternity houses and home again. And the toys you provided; lifted trucks, cars, a boat, jet skis, surfboards, motorcycles, quads, classic cars, and a fun vacation home. Some might say we spoiled our kids. You always said that they were our kids, and we will raise them as we want.

You worked so hard to build a life for our family. The kids always felt safe because they knew you had their back no matter what. They are learning that as adults, they don't need Dad's safety net. They just have to believe in themselves.

You would be so proud of Kris, Cory, Dani, our daughters-in-law, Erin and Kelley, our soon-to-be son-in-law, Mike, and your sweet, like daughter Mandy. They have survived the unimaginable pain of losing their dad, father-in-law, and Papa G. They've had to face the reality that you took your own life without warning or any reasonable explanation. They live with so many unanswered questions and continue to be vulnerable to uninformed comments and speculations from friends because of the shame suicide leaves behind. Your death will be part of their story and my story forever. But it will not define us, and it will not break us. It sucks, and it hurts, but one split second of irrational behavior does not erase the man, father, husband, or friend you were.

You taught Kris and Cory more than they thought. Together, they have found their footing in the business and continue to amaze me each day. They have met every challenge professionally and successfully. When needed, they've leaned on critical vendors, asked questions, made tough decisions, solidified relationships with key customers, managed difficult employees, and admitted mistakes made. They've done this without you at the helm. Without you pulling a miracle out of your ass, and without you to give them an "atta-boy." They do it to honor the gift you left them.

And Dani, our sweet, precious, beautiful baby girl, you would be so proud of her. You know she is a mixture of both of us, with your drive, ambition, work ethic, and the desire to be the best at what she does and with my heart and compassion. Dani wanted and needed to be close to me this past year. I am so grateful because I needed her, too. Our home is not a comfortable place for the boys, especially Kris. But Dani finds comfort in being at home.

Erin, Kelley, and Mike have consistently been the "silent heroes" by loving Cory, Kris, and Dani through the most difficult time they have faced as couples. I don't ever forget the challenges they face daily, watching the love of their life grieve and not knowing exactly what to say or how to help—working through their Grief silently and trying to explain the unexplainable to their own families and friends. They watch our kids elevate you to hero status one day and lash out at you in anger the next. Kris and Kelley have faced extra challenges while grieving, including infertility. Cory and Erin, as new parents, balance the daily joys of raising their son, Colt, with the sadness of knowing Colt will most likely not remember you. Dani and Mike have dealt with Grief in the midst of planning a wedding and their future together.

And sweet, sweet Mandy. The one we chose to love as our own. You loved teasing her about the boys she would date, and you loved it when she would tease you back about your mullet. Mandy was the one who named you Papa G for all of eternity. Mandy has the extra burden of finding her place in the family's Grief, not wanting to step on anyone's feelings, especially Dani's. Mandy is Dani's person, wifey, and BFF, but she is also the one whom the entire Glidden family chose to bring into the fold. Her Grief is valid.

Our adorable grandson, Colt Grayson, is one of God's most beautiful examples of God's perfect timing. Colt isn't old enough to understand the significance of what happened a year ago. In Colt's world, nothing has changed. Colt doesn't treat us differently or ask questions we can't or don't want to answer. He is pure, uncensored, unplugged love, and he fills my cup and refreshes my soul. I looked forward to every Wednesday when I watch Colt because I can relax and just be for eight hours.

One year later, our entire family and circle of friends still can't believe you are gone. My Mom and Dad miss you so much. They grieve your loss, and they weep for us. Hawk has chosen to spend today in Havasu alone, sitting in your chair and smoking a cigar. Some of our friends and close business associates still shed a tear when thinking about you. They, too, are hurting.

All of us have done a remarkable job picking up the pieces one by one and moving forward. It's not fair, and I would not wish this pain on anyone. But this is life. We are family, and together we will come through this heartache, better, wiser, and more compassionate.

I have never experienced the kind of pain I have felt this past year, but my blessings far outweigh the pain. You, our kids, my friends, and my family *are my most glorious blessings, and nothing will ever take that away from me, not even death. I am secure in knowing that you are in Heaven, free from back pain, sleep problems, prostate cancer side effects, and worry. No tears, no sadness, just peace. I will always love you, Mr. G.*

Love,
Marci[7]

We survived the first year—the year of firsts.

OUR DAUGHTER'S WEDDING

We hosted an engagement party for our daughter, Dani, and her fiancé Mike, at our home in July 2014, three weeks before Paul died. That was the last time Dani saw her dad. Our beautiful baby girl, weeks into dreaming and planning for her wedding day, now has to share her joyous heart with Grief.

My journal entry - 6/3/2015: I am so angry! I don't understand, Paul. Why now? You were at both our sons' weddings! But you're not going to be there for Dani—our baby girl? You won't be here to walk her down the aisle or give a funny speech or have that Father/Daughter dance????? I am so pissed![8]

I poured my energy into Dani's wedding, determined to give her all she wanted and more. I knew I couldn't make up for her dad not being there, but I was determined to make it the best day possible under the circumstances. I also knew that our guests would be nervously anticipating some critical moments during the wedding and reception, and those moments would be glaringly absent of Paul's sarcastic wit and laughter. This wedding should be a joyous and beautiful day for Dani and Mike, filled with tears of joy and not sadness.

I'm not only the Mother of the Bride but also the fill-in Father of the Bride. Impossible shoes to fill in three critical moments in a wedding. Who will walk Dani down the aisle? The obvious answer is her two brothers, Kris and Cory, but it would be too hard for me to watch. I felt it would be equally difficult for our guests. I wanted to do something bigger and bolder. So, instead of just her brothers, Kris and Cory, walking her down the aisle, I asked eight men to walk with her. One brother on each side of her, followed by a grandfather, four uncles, and Paul's best friend, Hawk. And when asked, "Who gives this woman to this man?" All eight men said, "WE DO!" Our guests responded with laughter and smiles.

I gave what should have been the Father of the Bride speech. I wrote a short book about our daughter and how she met and fell in love with Mike. After acknowledging Paul's absence and how much he looked forward to this day, I asked our guests to indulge me as I read my daughter one last bedtime story. As I read the book, I presented a photographic slide show of Dani and Mike. I included Paul's picture and talked about how honored Paul was when Mike asked his permission to marry Dani. It was bittersweet.

And when it was time for the traditional Father and Daughter dance, I told Dani I would join her on the dance floor, and the two of us would dance with her brothers. Secretly, I asked girlfriends and other important women in Dani's life to join us on the dance floor when they heard the D.J. play "I Feel Like a Woman!" And they did. Women were dancing around the bride, laughing and full of joy. Dani was a beautiful bride, and she enjoyed every magical moment of the day.

MOVING FORWARD

I loved my house before August 13, 2014. Paul and I had spent several years remodeling areas of the house to fit our tastes and lifestyle. We reconfigured a staircase, replaced flooring downstairs, arched doorways, added rustic beams to ceilings, refaced the fireplace, and replaced windows with glass doors. Our backyard was an entertainer's dream, complete with a pool, spa, and covered outdoor bar with a flat-screen TV. Admittedly, the house was too big for two people, but it was perfect for entertaining family and friends.

But emotionally, I couldn't live there anymore. After Dani's wedding, I started thinking about when and where I wanted to move. Looking for a new home was exciting most of the time. It would be the first time I purchased a home by myself. I could choose the floor plan, how many bedrooms and bathrooms, the size of the kitchen, and the neighborhood. All the excitement of planning and dreaming about a new house couldn't overcome the sadness I felt leaving my dream home. I kicked and screamed throughout the process.

As days moved forward, little by little, I started feeling hopeful about my future. I had more to give, more to do, and more love to share. In December 2015, I took my sons, daughters-in-law, daughter, and son-in-law to a nice dinner at a well-known restaurant in Newport Coast. I was nervous about telling them I wanted to explore the dating world because I didn't know how they would react. I believed they wanted to see me happy again, but I didn't know if they were ready to see me dating. I assured the kids I would be careful, and I would always let someone know where I was going and with whom. I reminded them they were not responsible for my happiness, and my dating experiences would be privately mine until I knew I was interested in someone they should meet. With smiles on their faces, they raised their glasses of champagne and said, "You go, Mom!"

If only it would be that easy.

CHAPTER 8

#TakeTwo

"You gave me a forever within the numbered days..."[1]
—**John Green,** *The Fault in Our Stars*

My journal entry –11/1/2015: Paul, I miss you and love you! I wish I could change this outcome, but I can't. I'm tired of just existing and surviving. I want to live. I don't know what my life will look like in a year, in five years, or ten years. You always told me that if something ever happened to you, I would find someone to love. I don't know if that's true. Who will love me? You took your own life. When I tell someone how you died, will he understand? I'm scared. What will the kids think? They say they want me happy, but do they? I don't want them to think I've forgotten about you, or I don't love you anymore.[2]

Grief doesn't include a static timetable. My decision to move forward was difficult, very personal, and appropriate timing for me. I did not leave forty years of loving Paul behind when I decided to walk on into my future. The love I shared with Paul and every shared experience is an integral part of who I am and who I will always be. I didn't stop loving Paul when he died, but I was no longer married to Paul. One phase of my life had abruptly ended; the most challenging then began.

DATING

I was scared, but at the same time, oddly excited about what the future held for me. I never believed I could fall in love again, but I wasn't ready to quit living. I hoped to find someone I could go out to dinner with, catch a movie, engage in stimulating conversation, and attend social events. I hadn't dated for over forty years, and so much had changed. I heard so many horror stories about online dating and people not being who they said they were. How could I protect myself from scams or predators?

How and where do I meet someone? I researched my options and decided to hire a matchmaking firm because they insisted on background checks on all participants before making matches. It was an expensive service, but I felt comfortable the matchmakers would pair me with dates based on compatibility in many areas. The downside to using this service is they did not provide a photo of matches. I forgot the importance of physical attraction when dating.

My first date through the matchmaking firm was with Steve, a gentleman sixty-two years old. He was a former professional basketball player with blue eyes and gray hair. We spoke on the phone several times before agreeing to meet for a drink in Laguna Beach at a restaurant near the boardwalk. I was nervous for days leading up to the date and considered canceling, but I wanted to get "the first date" out of the way. I needed to know it was possible to date, engage in conversation with a man, and enjoy spending time with a man without feelings of guilt and without throwing up from my nervousness.

My date with Steve was exciting and awkward. I enjoyed learning about Steve's career as a professional basketball player, but I wasn't fascinated with the details of his two failed marriages. About a half-hour into the date, I asked Steve why he was drinking only water. He said drinking alcohol became a problem in his last marriage. (Red Flag #1) WHAT? Why then did Steve suggest meeting for a drink if alcohol was a problem? So, I said, "Steve, why don't we walk up the street and finish our conversation over a cup of coffee?" And with that, we walked to the closest coffee shop and continued our conversation.

We both ordered coffee and sat down at a small table overlooking the Pacific Coast Highway. They delivered Steve's coffee to our table quickly, but my coffee never came. Steve continued talking about his successful painting business and name-dropping celebrity clients while never noticing I had not received my coffee. (Red Flag #2) I finally mentioned I didn't get my coffee and expected Steve to say something like, "I'm sorry. Let me find the waitress and ask about your coffee." Instead, Steve ignored my comment and kept talking. (Red Flag #3) I gained insight into Steve's character—boring and self-absorbed. Not my cup of tea—or coffee.

The matchmaking company suggested a second pairing with "Gary." He was funny, easy to talk to, and loved boating, so I agreed to meet Gary for dinner at a local restaurant. Gary had never married, and I quickly understood why. Too many red flags to count. I couldn't wait for dinner to end. In retrospect, I should have excused myself under the pretense of going to the restroom and ghosted. But that's not my nature, so I endured the evening through its conclusion.

I returned home after that date in tears, and Grief was waiting up for me. Grief asked, *"Marci, why have you been crying? You said you wanted to date. You told yourself you were ready."* I didn't want to have a conversation with Grief. Not now. Not tonight. I screamed, *"I hate this! Why did Paul leave me? My life will never be good again! I'll be alone for the rest of my life."* Grief said, *"Marci, Paul loved you."*

"He quit. He didn't love me enough to stay," I responded.

Two dates and I was ready to throw in the towel. All the funny, intelligent, compassionate, caring, loving men must be happily married or looking for women much younger. The two men I met represented what was left over. I was glad I didn't let anyone know I started dating. I could pretend those dates never happened and move forward alone.

My self-imposed pity party lasted for only a while, but I wasn't ready to live the rest of my life without love. The matchmaking company introduced me to a gentleman that lived in my community. His name was John, and he was a Securities and Exchange compliance attorney for a prominent investment firm and six years my junior. John was charming, handsome, and very smart, but he was also the father of a six-year-old son. Although John and I were close in age, we were in completely different stages of life. My kids were grown and married; his only child was in first grade. I asked John why he waited until his mid-forties to become a parent. I learned John typically dated much younger women, and he became a father following a "casual dating relationship" with a woman in her twenties.

After my date with John, I severed my relationship with the matchmaking service. I felt I had been taken advantage of and embarrassed I had paid so much money to a matchmaking service. I felt vulnerable for the first time. How had I fallen for their pitch? I thought I didn't have the "wherewithal" or "know it all" to compete in the dating market. Losing your husband to suicide takes a significant hit on your self-esteem and self-worth. After my first three dates, I felt defeated. I questioned my worthiness to date, my attractiveness, and my ability to believe I could have a beautiful life after Paul.

My journal entry – 12/18/2016: Dating sucks! I want my life back! I want to be Paul's wife again! I'm so embarrassed and so discouraged. Will I feel this bad—every day—for the rest of my life?[3]

Living with Grief is exhausting. Grief is akin to an annoying roommate that won't move out. The roommate who wants to talk when I want to be left alone. The roommate is always at home when I'm desperate for privacy. The roommate that reminds me of the life I once knew and loved is gone. Despite Grief invading every aspect of my life, I still desired to live again and love again. Tom Zuba, life coach and author of *Permission to Mourn*, describes the push and pull of the voices in your head: *"And the truth is you have two voices in your head. And it feels like these two voices do battle every day. One voice tells you that you will be okay. That you will be happy again. That you can do this. That you have the courage, the strength, the knowledge, the wisdom, the grace to live again. And the other voice says, No. It is too scary out there. You will be hurt again. You will not recover. It is not possible. The sorrow is too deep. The loss too great. You are doomed to a life of pain, of sadness, of suffering, of isolation of desperation."*[4]

It would be my choice, and mine alone, which voice I chose to follow.

I prayed there was a bigger plan for my life, even though I couldn't see it. I decided to try the dating world again. I did something I thought I would never do—I signed up with an online dating service. And I told no one. I signed up for a thirty-day trial period, filled out my first and only dating profile, uploaded one photo, and pressed *send*. Within an hour, I received several comments from men interested in my profile and one insensitive comment from a creep reprimanding me for only posting one photo. What? Who is this jerk, and why did he feel the need to harass me over posting one photo? I pulled up his profile and re-read his comments. He suggested I only posted one picture because I don't look like this photo anymore. Didn't I know that a "one-photo profile" was not considered legitimate and often dismissed in the online dating world?

I fired off a response to the gentleman who called me out. More or less, I replied, *"Whoa…I don't appreciate your condescending tone. You don't know me, and you certainly don't know my backstory. Today is the first time I have ever been on any dating site. I was happily married for almost thirty-five years to the love of my life until August 2014, when my husband took his own life. You can't begin to know what I have gone through or the challenges I faced in the last eighteen months. I lost the only man I have ever loved. I'm trying to rebuild my life one day at a time. So, excuse me if I didn't know the rules for posting photos on dating websites."* To my surprise, the gentleman apologized for his comments. He was sorry for my loss and hoped I would accept his apology. We chatted back and forth a few times and wished each other success in finding a future partner.

Online dating is scary. I've heard horror stories about online predators, people providing false profile details, women pretending to be men and vice versa, and people misrepresenting their current appearance by posting photos taken years ago. If I met someone, how could I trust they would be who they said they are? I didn't have a long dating resume. My dating experience started and ended in high school. I was seventeen the last time I used my flirting skills. The good news is online dating can be oddly empowering. Like other social media platforms, you communicate through laptops, iPad, and cellphones with as much anonymity as you need and want. You can spend hours peering into the lives of available dating candidates, reading profiles, and sifting through photos without their knowledge. You can disregard the winks or waves or flirtatious emoticons with a few keystrokes on your laptop.

I love the idea of love. I enjoy loving and being loved by someone. That's who I am. Loving is an intrinsic characteristic of mine. I wasn't trying to replace Paul. Paul was irreplaceable. I wasn't looking for a man to support me or complete me. I was hoping to find a smart, caring, funny man and enjoyed going to dinner, a movie, or a concert. A man capable of acknowledging with compassion and respect the circumstances which caused me to be a widow. I also hoped I wouldn't need to keep my dating life a secret forever. And if by chance, I connected with someone, he would be received warmly and positively by my children, family, and friends.

A SECOND CHANCE AT LOVE

A few days later, I received a wink and a quick hello as a conversation starter from a man named Michael. I liked his profile pictures and his profile. He was six foot five, with green eyes and a hint of short gray hair appropriately allowed to grow in some areas of his bald head. He also had a great smile. His profile pictures ranged from him suited up and participating at corporate events to zip-lining and traveling internationally. He indicated he was separated, and his wife lived out of state. Divorce proceedings would begin as soon as his wife relocated closer to her family. I was surprised at his honesty about being separated. He could have easily said he was divorced, but he didn't. He was looking for someone that enjoyed laughter, life, and holding hands. So, I responded!

We emailed back and forth for a few weeks getting to know each other a bit before he asked me if I would consider meeting him for a drink some night. He was out of town visiting family for the holidays, but he suggested a restaurant we were both familiar with to meet at 7:00 p.m. on January 1. Before he ended the conversation, he said, "By the way, I want you to know my name is Michael Savage. If you don't feel comfortable telling me your full name, I understand. But I wanted you to know mine." I didn't tell Michael my full name; I decided to meet him first out of an abundance of caution. However, now I had his full name and the name of the company he worked for to locate him on LinkedIn.

We met as planned at the restaurant on January 1, 2016. I arrived first, so I watched Michael get out of his car and walk toward me. He was very tall, very well dressed and very handsome! Michael held the door for me as we entered and followed just behind me as the hostess led us to a table at the bar. He pulled out the chair for me and waited until I was seated before he sat down. I was thinking to myself, "His mama raised him right!" We started talking, and before I knew it, three hours had come and gone. Michael was easy to communicate with, and I enjoyed his laughter. I was interested in how he talked about his maternal grandparents and how much time he spent with them as a child. I spent a lot of time with my grandparents when I was young, so I related to why Michael's grandparents were vital to him. We commiserated about how difficult it was dating at this age, and Michael shared a few stories about some crazy dates he experienced.

Michael and I discussed what happened to put us both in a place to be dating. I was truthful about Paul's death and how painful the aftermath had been. Michael talked about his choices and decisions, which contributed to his marriage failing, and why he and his wife separated two years ago. We found common ground in many areas and laughed about our differences in music and politics. I thanked Michael for a beautiful evening as he walked me to my car. Before I opened my car door, I turned to Michael, thanked him again, and told him I enjoyed our time together.

He looked at me and asked, "Can I kiss you?"

I smiled and said, "I would like that."

That was the second time in my life I ever kissed someone on the first date; the first time was with Paul. We stood in the parking lot next to my car, talking and kissing. Time seemed to stand still, and everything and everyone around us disappeared. I wanted to stand in that parking lot until the sun came up, but I reluctantly said, "I have to go home."

Michael asked, "Why?"

I smiled and said, "Because I'm a lady. That's why!"

As I drove away, I watched him in my rearview mirror and giggled out loud like a young schoolgirl with a crush. Over and over, I kept thinking, What just happened? I was surprised at how I felt. It was so good to be kissed, held, and to know a man was interested and attracted to me. Michael texted me when I got home and asked me if I would go to dinner with him the next night. I probably should have hesitated for a hot minute or two or declined the invitation and said I already had plans—to see how he reacted or if he would call me again. But at this age, there is no time for games. I wanted to see him also, so I said yes.

Michael asked, "Would you like me to pick you up, or would you feel more comfortable meeting me at the restaurant?"

I responded, "Ummmm…what do you think?"

Michael chuckled, "Well if we meet at the restaurant, it makes for an awkward kiss later in the valet line."

Laughing, I said, "I'll text you my address. Oh, and by the way, my last name is Glidden."

The next day, Michael texted me the name of the beachside restaurant we would be dining at, and the time he would pick me up. He also sent several other texts with funny and romantic one-liners from well-known movies or songs during the day. It was a bit corny but sweet and sentimental. I thought, okay, two can play this game. I called the restaurant and told them I was having dinner with Mr. Savage at seven and asked the concierge to put a note on our table which said "right place, right time" and have a bottle of champagne chilled for us.

Michael arrived on time to pick me up with flowers in hand and, believe it or not, a bottle of champagne. When we arrived at the restaurant and sat down, Michael noticed the letter and champagne. Great minds think alike.

He whispered, "I think they sat us at someone else's table."

I said, "No, this is our table, and the note and champagne are from me to you."

He looked at me in disbelief and said, "For me? You called ahead and had this done for me? Marci, it's usually expected to be all about the woman, not the man in the dating world. That was incredibly nice of you, and you didn't need to do it, but it means a great deal to me."

I smiled and said, "I don't know how the dating world works these days, but I know how successful relationships work. I was in one for almost forty years. Two people need to be vested in the relationship if it's going to work and stand the test of time. It can never be a one-way street."

The following week, Michael had a four-day business trip planned, so he asked me to meet for dinner again before he left. At dinner, Michael said, "Paul must have been an amazing man." The comment caught me off guard.

I replied, "Yes, Paul was an amazing man. What made you say that?"

Michael smiled and said, "You're not the only one who can do a little research by Googling a name."

After I told Michael my last name, he Googled me, and the website my friend launched in honor of Paul popped up, and Michael watched Paul's memorial service. Michael thought it was a beautiful memorial, and he could tell how much I loved Paul. It felt good to know that Michael had taken the time to watch the video and acknowledged the love I had for Paul.

Our conversation over dinner moved beyond fun and flirtatious to more thoughtful questions about where do we go from here? Michael and I had an undeniable attraction to each other and wanted to know if there could be more beyond the physical chemistry. Michael asked me if I would be interested in suspending our online dating sites and seeing where a relationship between us would go. Neither one of us had expectations of a serious relationship, but we were both open to the possibility of what could be and investing the time to get to know each other. And so, it began.

In the beginning, my sister Nikki and my daughter-in-law Kelley were the only two people who knew I was dating Michael. I struggled with keeping Michael a secret for long; I wanted to share my excitement with my Bunco Babes. It felt so good to wake up in the mornings and know I could feel happy again. I could feel the sunshine instead of a gray, foggy cloud permeating my every thought and action. I didn't know what the future held, but for the first time since August 13, 2014, I believed there could be a future for me. I could live again and not just survive or exist. A few weeks into dating Michael, I shared my news with my Bunco girlfriends at our monthly dinner. I sensed their happiness and concerns about my vulnerability as a widow entering the dating world.

My girlfriend, Sheree, said, "Marci, please be careful!"

I responded, "Sheree, I'll be careful. I'm having fun, and if Michael and I last another two weeks or two years, I'll be okay. I've already had the worst thing happen to me; I can't hurt more than that."

My words that night haunt me to this day; I didn't know lightning would strike the same place twice.

Michael was four years younger than me and had two children. His son was finishing his last college semester, and his daughter was beginning her senior year in college. Michael had lived in Orange County for just over a year. He relocated from the Chicago area to accept a job with a globally recognized connectors manufacturer for various industries. Michael had been married for over twenty-five years and separated for the past two years. The company provided a relocation package, and Michael chose to use the relocation benefit to help his wife move to Colorado. Once she settled, divorce proceedings would begin. Michael's separation and pending divorce was painful for me, especially as time passed, and I enjoyed Michael's company more and more.

IT'S TIME TO INTRODUCE MICHAEL

After dating Michael for a month, I thought it was time to tell my kids about him. The more time I spent with Michael, the more I wanted to integrate Michael into every aspect of my life and introduce him to the most important people in my life—my children. After dinner at my house one night, I asked my kids and their spouses to grab a drink and join me by the fire pit in the backyard. I hoped they would accept my news and be happy for me. I remembered the dinner before Christmas a few months back and the toast they proposed with excitement when I told them I was ready to move forward. However, what came next was unexpected. My children reacted with surprise, apprehension, and skepticism. They were no longer excited as they were at Christmas. At the time, the evening felt like a disaster. Now I see it not as a disaster but as a gut-wrenching display of pain and Grief left in the hearts of loved ones in the wake of an uncommon loss. The first challenge I faced in my new chapter of life was accepting that my children's Grief was different from mine.

Michael and I knew our relationship would not be without challenges. The divorce rate for second marriages is around 60% higher than the divorce rate for first marriages. Although our children are all adults, blending families can be challenging. We met each other's children, family, and friends and remained respectful of each other's first marriages, allowing the other to talk openly and proudly about past love and experiences. Michael was different from Paul in many ways; being attracted to the differences did not negate my love for Paul. I struggled with finding the right words and the appropriate way to explain that attraction to my children. I constantly rewrote statements in my head before saying something or withdrew from saying anything at all. I didn't want my children to overanalyze something I said or misinterpret the tone in which it was delivered. Causing them more pain was the last thing I intended or desired.

Michael's cousin Dave has been a widower for several years. We've had a couple of opportunities to discuss the challenges we face moving forward after losing our spouses. We each have two sons and a daughter. I asked Dave how his children felt about him dating, and did they all feel the same? Dave said they all reacted very differently. One child was on board about him dating, one child was analytical about the process, and one child opposed the idea. I laughed a little and said my three were all different as well. During our phone conversation, Dave said something I will never forget.

Dave said, "Marci, isn't it wonderful how the soul can regenerate itself, and at our age, you can feel eighteen years old or twenty-one or twenty-five all over again?"

I said, "Yes, it is!"

Michael was the first to say he was in love. I would always tell Michael I loved him, but he knew I couldn't completely give my heart to him until he was divorced. He understood and respected my feelings. And Michael and I agreed to respect our past marriages. Both of Michael's children graduated from college during the first year we dated. Michael wanted me to join him at his kids' graduations, but I refused to go. I knew it would be disrespectful and inappropriate for me to attend. His son and daughter's college graduations should be focused solely on their accomplishments and celebrated as a family.

Michael encouraged my kids to talk about Paul openly in his presence. Sometimes, I felt my kids weren't accepting my dating Michael as quickly as I expected. Michael would say to me, "Marci, be patient. They lost their dad, and this is hard for them. I understand and respect their hesitation." Michael also knew I had friends and other family members suspicious of his reasons for dating me. Michael would remind me, "Marci, your friends don't know me very well. You need to give them time to get to know me and see that I love you, and I'm not dating you for your money or your business." I admired Michael's respect for my family and friends. He never had a bad word to say about anyone.

Michael and I talked about what we were looking for in a relationship, including our expectations and limitations. With two children in college, his living expenses, and supporting his estranged wife, who did not work, Michael had very little discretionary income. I could help myself, and I wasn't looking for a man to support me financially. When we traveled, we purchased our airfare separately and split the accommodations and other travel-related expenses. Michael insisted on always paying for our date nights unless I wanted to surprise him or plan something special for his birthday. Setting boundaries in our relationship at the beginning freed us up to enjoy our time together and embrace life. We enjoyed trying new restaurants, attending music concerts, going to the movies, sitting on the beach while drinking a glass of wine, BBQing at home, watching Netflix, or spontaneously deciding to pack an overnight bag and take a road trip.

My journal entry –March 17, 2017: Michael's divorce was final. It was the first day I felt free to say to Michael, "I love you."[5]

PARIS, ITALY, AND A PROPOSAL

Michael's employer planned to exhibit at the annual Paris Air Show in June the same year. Although Michael would be working at the air show, he invited me to join him. He thought I could explore Paris during the day while he worked, and we would have the evenings and the weekend to enjoy Paris together. Michael also invited me to vacation with him in Italy the week before Paris. I had never been to Europe and was so excited about the opportunity to see Italy and Paris with Michael.

Before our European vacation and without my knowledge, Michael had dinner with my three kids, Kris, Cory, and Dani, and told them he planned to ask me to marry him while we were in Italy, and he wanted their blessing. Michael assured my kids he was in love with me and was not interested in our family business or replacing Paul, and he and I would put together a prenuptial agreement before getting married. I heard it was a good dinner; Michael encouraged my kids to ask tough questions and voice any concerns about their mom remarrying.

In Italy, we stayed in a boutique hotel on the Arno river for three nights in Florence and four nights at an Airbnb in a vineyard in San Gimignano in Tuscany. Michael enjoyed photography and planned to take a photography lesson with Italian photographers in Florence. The photographers would guide us on a tour of famous places in the city and give Michael an experience in photographing architecture. We met the two photographers at the Piazzale Michelangelo, a well-known destination for tourists who wanted to photograph Florence's skyline. Michael's photography lesson started there and continued as we walked up to the basilica San Miniato al Monte just above the Piazzale.

After Michael and the photographers finished photographing the inside of the basilica, Michael and I walked out to the plaza, and Michael said, "Marci, let's stop here and enjoy the view for a few minutes." Then Michael dropped down on one knee, pulled out a ring from his pocket, and proposed. I started crying and said, "Yes, Michael, of course, I'll marry you!" Michael did not hire the photographers for a private photography lesson; he hired them to photograph the proposal. It was one of the most romantic moments in my life, and I felt so thankful I had a second chance to love again and be loved.

In Paris, we stayed at the same hotel with his business colleagues working the air show. When it was over, we moved to a boutique hotel in another area of Paris. We spent three days exploring Paris together as a newly engaged couple, including a guided tour of the Louvre, a private wine tasting in the Louver's cellar, an all-day recommended food tour, a riverboat cruise on the Seine, and a romantic dinner overlooking the Eiffel Tower. I didn't want the vacation to end, but I was excited to plan our wedding and begin our life as Mr. and Mrs. Savage.

NEW LOVE, NEW FUTURE, NEW DREAMS

I didn't expect ever to find joy and love again, but I did. So many people commented on how different I looked. They could see how happy and at peace I was and how much I loved Michael. And vice versa. Michael was equally in love with me. My family and friends were relieved to see me happy again, and Michael's family and friends felt the same. A beautiful love affair on the threshold of a new beginning. Our friend Kevin once said, "It's hard to find love on the back nine." Yes, it's hard, but not impossible.

Surrounded by friends and family, Michael and I married on July 7, 2018. It was a beautiful wedding, a fantastic start to our second chance at love. A few days later, we flew to Providenciales Island in the Turks and Caicos for our honeymoon. Ten glorious days relaxing on the beach, traversing the beautiful turquoise Caribbean water on private boat charters, horseback riding, and dining on the beach at sunset. I'm so thankful we had that time together. It turned out to be our last vacation together—ever.

CHAPTER 9

March 15, 2019

"The risk of love is loss, and the price of loss is Grief.
But the pain of Grief is only a shadow when
compared with the pain of never risking love."
–Hilary Stanton Zunin

When I met Michael in January 2016, he was an executive within the Aerospace and Defense division of a major U.S. corporation. Because Michael's employer engineered and manufactured various connectors used by the military, the company undergoes a rigorous qualification process through the Defense Logistics Agency (DLA) to be a qualified supplier. The DLA is our nation's combat logistics support agency managing the global supply chain of various products used by the Army, Marine Corps, Navy, Air Force, Space Force, Coast Guard, multiple commands, and other federal agencies. Michael told me his employer had recently been removed from the Qualified Supplier list and underwent a lengthy requalification process. A few months after meeting Michael, his employer began restructuring the executive management team of his division, and the first to be let go was the Chief Executive Officer.

The President of the Aerospace and Defense division took the role of interim CEO. When there is a significant change to a company's leadership team, employees often analyze the difference and start thinking about how it will affect their position. The interim CEO had been with the company for over ten years and was a likely candidate for CEO permanently. Requalification for the Qualified Supplier List by the DLA was the top priority for the interim CEO. The entire executive team and their direct reports worked diligently over the next two years to be re-qualified and put new procedures to assure future compliance.

TEETERING ON THE EDGE

On May 21, 2018, the company terminated Michael, the Director of Operations, and the Director of Engineering. Michael was disappointed but not surprised. He had been in the industry for over thirty years and lived through several corporate reorganizations. At fifty-seven, Michael knew it would be difficult to find employment comparable to his current position and salary level. Michael had substantial financial obligations following his divorce in March 2017. Following divorce mediation, Michael agreed to divide all marital assets equally and pay alimony until he turned sixty-five. In addition to his regular monthly living expenses, Michael had other substantial and unresolved financial obligations. And Michael was marrying me in forty-seven days.

Before our wedding, Michael and I signed a premarital agreement. Having a prenup going into a second marriage is common and usually suggested. We both had children from our previous marriages, and we agreed our children should benefit from any assets we acquired individually before our wedding. Once married, we decided to keep our finances completely separate, including filing individual tax returns. Michael and I married because we loved each other and wanted to be together. Neither one of us looked to the other for financial support at that time, but hindsight is 20/20. I now believe the economic inequity between Michael and myself slowly chipped away at his self-worth.

TIME IS OF THE ESSENCE

Michael had always dreamed of starting his own business, and he believed the timing was right to pursue his dream. Michael reconnected with a former colleague, now the CEO of a relatively new connectors manufacturer in South America. The South American manufacturer had experienced steady growth in the first four years due to their connectors' low cost. The company had sales representation for the South American and European markets, but none in North America. Michael inquired about the possibility of representing them in the North American market. Michael had over thirty years of experience to offer in the connector business. But Michael didn't know if the South American connectors' quality could pass the rigorous testing required for the US marketplace or if the company was financially stable to assume an expansion. In mid-June 2018, Michael flew to South America to meet with the executive team and tour their manufacturing facility. Michael told me he was impressed with their facility and the quality of connectors they sold in Europe and Asia. The South American company agreed Michael could represent their connectors in North America. However, they couldn't reach an exclusivity agreement. Another rep in Florida wanted exclusive rights to sell the South American connectors, so the company suggested Michael meet the other broker and discuss working together.

Before returning home, Michael met with potential US investors to discuss this new venture. Michael could not fund a startup company. He needed capital to start his business and sustain the company for at least a year. The investors had known Michael for over twenty years and recognized his potential for success. They agreed to invest the necessary startup expenses and cover Michael's salary for one year in exchange for forty percent of the business. Once Michael secured financial investors, he contacted the other sales rep in Florida to discuss a partnership. Like Michael, the sales rep had been in the connector business for many years and had many contacts. However, the sales rep enjoyed full-time employment. He agreed to work with Michael as long as he could remain a silent partner until their company could afford his salary.

After Michael and I returned from our honeymoon in late July 2018, Michael and his silent partner signed a formal agreement with the connector company for exclusive North America representation. In early August 2018, Michael and the South American connector manufacturer's CEO met with several potential North American customers, including Michael's former employer. Michael's former employer was sourcing a connector; they currently did not manufacture and agreed to look at the South American company's connectors. Michael was very excited about potential business and told me he submitted the documentation required to become an approved vendor and supplied several connectors for testing, the accompanying CAD (computer-aided design) drawings of each connector, and the cost. Michael's former employer also sent representatives to tour the South American manufacturing facility and conduct a physical inspection required for new vendor approval.

Michael worked on this project with his former employer for almost six months. Michael told me he received an email on January 28, 2019, from an executive with his former employer stating they chose to go in a different direction on the project. Michael was to cease all communication with company employees. On January 29, 2019, Michael did communicate via text message with an employee who worked on the project. In the text Michael showed me how the employee indicated he did not know why upper management canceled the project, and he was "blown away with the abrupt decision."

Michael was disappointed in the loss of potential business after working on this project for so long. Losing this opportunity was a setback for Michael's new startup company. A week later, Michael's investors pulled back on the amount of funding they initially agreed to fund. Michael knew his startup company would run out of funds by the end of April. Michael's concern was bridging the gap financially from April to December 2019, when several customers' purchase orders were due.

Michael and his silent partner were in discussions with another potential investor, a respected industry leader with a global distribution network. A partnership with this investor would immediately put Michael's company in a firm financial standing and provide additional sales support, warehousing, and distribution capabilities. Michael organized a meeting with the potential investors for Monday, March 18, 2019.

THE BEGINNING OF THE END

Thursday, March 7

When I arrived home after work, I found Michael sitting at the kitchen bar, reading his mail. I asked him how his day had been, and Michael said, "Great until I got home and opened this letter from an attorney." An attorney hired by one of Michael's former employers sent the letter accusing Michael of contacting one of his former employer's customers.

Friday, March 8

Michael contacted the attorney, as requested in the letter. The attorney claimed his client knew of text messages between Michael and one of their employees, wherein Michael implied his intent to contact a former employer's current customer. Michael called his corporate attorney for advice at my urging, but she recommended a top business attorney for

Michael to get because she mainly dealt with contract law. Michael contacted the recommended attorney and emailed the letter and his severance documents to the business attorney. After the attorney reviewed the materials, he agreed to represent Michael. The attorney scheduled a meeting with Michael for Friday, March 15, at 1:00 p.m. to discuss the next steps. In the meantime, the attorney suggested Michael email the attorney and request in writing what his client wanted to avoid legal action. Michael followed his advice.

Saturday, March 9 - Sunday, March 10

With Michael's permission, I reached out to a personal friend who is a well-respected Intellectual Property attorney in San Diego, California, for a second opinion on how Michael should proceed. Michael and the attorney discussed the probable reasons behind a multi-million-dollar corporation threatening legal action against a former employee's startup company. They also discussed the State of California's stance regarding non-compete clauses. The attorney suggested Michael retain the business lawyer in Orange County to initiate dialogue with the opposing attorney. The best scenario is always to avoid legal action if possible and negotiate an agreement between parties from the start.

Monday, March 11

Michael reached out to his US investors requesting them to reconsider their position and continue their funding agreement until Michael could find additional funding. Michael hated asking. He texted me, "I hate I cannot fund this myself…I feel like I worked for thirty years and have nothing to show for my effort."

I responded to Michael's text, "You have a lifetime of experiences, lived in many places in the U.S., traveled and lived internationally, worked in high-level executive positions in huge corporations, provided for your family on one income, educated two amazing children, and on and on! That's what you have to show for thirty years of working experience!!! You have to stop being so hard on yourself!!! Have you forgotten you dodged the bullet on a fatal heart attack six months ago by catching your blockages early??? Perhaps you have also forgotten you are a newlywed, and your wife loves you and wants to grow old with you."

Michael texted back, "I haven't forgotten, and I know how blessed I am with you and my children in my life. I haven't forgotten how you have made my life so perfect. When the company pulled the program from us, I knew that we didn't have the funding to get through."

Tuesday, March 12

Michael received the agenda for the meeting with the investor scheduled for Monday, March 18. Michael wanted to be fully prepared for the discussion and continued working on his pitch deck. Later in the day, Michael sent me a screenshot of an email from his former employer's attorney. It read, "It is [Name of Company]'s understanding of your initial response to my letter that you are not and do not intend to interfere with [Name of Company]'s business and opportunities. If that understanding is not accurate, please let me know immediately, and we will take appropriate action. If it is accurate, please confirm in writing by close of business tomorrow."

Wednesday, March 13

Michael updates his silent partner and the South American connector manufacturer on the attorney's response. They both wanted Michael to make the problem go away. Any threat of legal action could jeopardize negotiations with potential investors. Michael scheduled a phone conference with his personal, corporate attorney, and business attorney for 8:30 p.m.

Michael took the call using the speaker on his phone, allowing me to hear the conversation and take notes. The business attorney laid out a possible scenario if legal action was necessary and the costs associated. Michael kept shaking his head in disbelief as we listened. The business attorney required a ten-thousand-dollar retainer before meeting with Michael on Friday, March 15. The attorney agreed that initiating dialogue with the opposing attorney to find a compromise would be a win for both parties. If the former employer wanted to pursue legal action, the next step would be gathering as much discovery as possible—gaining access to [Name of Company]'s emails, taking depositions from their employees and from customers of [Name of Company] whom they believed Michael would "interfere with their business and opportunities." The discovery process could cost as much as $200,000. If Michael's attorney needed to push further and prepare for trial, the cost could be another $200,000. The attorney reminded Michael, a case like this one could be continued and postponed for years.

Michael felt defeated and convinced his former employer was trying to keep him from competing. Michael said, "For almost six months, they vetted the manufacturer for approved supplier status, requested multiple samples of the product, asked for CAD drawings of the product, and requested my pricing structure. Then abruptly, they discontinue our relationship. They didn't even return our drawings or all the samples. I'm one man with a startup company trying to earn a living. I feel like they are trying to shut down my business."

I responded, "I don't know, baby. It doesn't make sense."

After the phone conference with the attorneys, Michael said he had something to give me. He asked me to close my eyes and hold out my hands. When I opened my eyes, I recognized the brown box from my favorite jeweler, David Yurman. Inside was a beautiful ring. I started to cry and said, "Oh, Michael, I can't accept this. You can't afford to buy me a ring right now." Michael smiled and told me he had the ring for weeks and waited for a special moment to give it to me. He admitted he purchased the DY ring from a private party and not from the store. The ring didn't fit, so Michael promised to get the ring resized for me. I told Michael that the story behind this ring meant more to me than if he had walked into the store and bought it new.

Thursday, March 14

I reminded Michael of my monthly Bunco dinner with my girlfriends and told Michael I would be home around ten in the evening. Before I left dinner with my girlfriends, Michael texted me, "I got a positive email from the CEO of the company interested in investing. He gave me a very well-thought-out list of elements to discuss the investment!! He would never put this lengthy agenda and questions together if they weren't interested. I may need to talk to my attorney to understand some of the parts. But I can tell they want to be partners. He put a lot of work into this, and I like where he is going with the approach. It made me very happy!!!!!!!"

When I got home, Michael seemed less stressed and very hopeful for his meeting on Monday. I was pleasantly surprised to see Michael attempting to make himself dinner. He put a ribeye steak in the smoker but fell asleep on the couch and burned the meat. We had a good laugh about Michael searing the steak because he was an extraordinary cook and used the smoker four to five times each week. We went to bed together that night, as we always did. Michael read for a while on his iPad and then cuddled up next to me and held me as we fell asleep.

Friday, March 15

Michael and I woke up as usual and went through our routine, getting ready for work. Before we left the house, Michael asked me to give him the David Yurman ring, so he could take it to a jeweler and have it resized for me. He winked and said, "I have to go to the jeweler anyway. I've been working on your birthday gift." I smiled and handed him the ring. We hugged and kissed, and I said, "Call me or text me after you meet with the attorney. I know he will help clear up this issue. Stay focused on your meeting on Monday with the investor. Don't forget we have dinner with Dani and Mike tonight at 6:00. I love you!"

THE FINAL STRAW

When I arrived at work, I found a large package on my desk addressed to Michael. Michael used my office address for business correspondence instead of our home address. I didn't recognize the sender's name, so I Googled the name and address—it was a law office. I called Michael and informed him of the package. He asked me to open it and let him know what it contained.

The envelope contained a cease and desist demand letter prepared by a law firm representing another of Michael's former employers. The letter also named Michael's silent partner and the South American manufacturer. Michael was quiet as I read the letter to him over the phone. I asked him if he wanted to pick up the documents at my office before he met with the attorney at 1:00 or did he want me to scan the documents to his office. Michael replied, "Scan me the documents." Before I hung up the phone, I said, "Baby, something doesn't smell right about all of this. What are the chances of you receiving two letters threatening legal action from two of your former employers in the same week? Didn't you once tell me that these two companies do business together? Where I'm from, someone might say, "'This dog don't hunt.'" Your attorney needs to read these documents." I scanned the documents to Michael at his office in Irvine. Michael emailed me back, "Thank you, sweetheart. Everything will be okay."

I had a hair appointment at the same time as Michael's appointment with his attorney. I kept my phone in my lap, anticipating Michael's text message after his meeting, but he never texted me. When I left the hair salon, I called Michael, but he didn't answer. So, I texted him, "Are you still with the attorney? I'm leaving the hair salon and on my way home. Baby, please call me! What time will you be home? Remember, we are having dinner at Dani and Mike's tonight at 6:00." No response from Michael was very unusual; Michael always responded.

I don't know why, but I knew something was wrong. I pulled into the driveway, opened the garage, and Michael's car wasn't there. I went into the house and started calling Michael's cell phone over and over again. Still no response. I became more anxious and scared as time passed, and I didn't hear from Michael. We had dinner plans with my daughter and son-in-law, so I called to apologize for the last-minute cancelation and explained that Michael wasn't home and I couldn't reach him. My daughter asked if I needed her help, and I said, "No. I'm sure there's a good reason, and Michael will call or show up soon."

After I hung up the phone, I decided to call the attorney Michael had a meeting with and ask what time the meeting concluded, but I realized I didn't have the attorney's name or contact information. I found Michael's personal attorney's phone number on his desk and called her. I explained to her my concerns because it was unusual for Michael not to respond to my calls or texts. She offered to contact the business attorney Michael had a scheduled meeting with earlier. Within minutes she called me back and said, "Michael called and canceled the meeting. He said a family emergency had come up." She knew the threat of legal action was stressful for Michael, and she thought perhaps Michael needed some time to himself to sort things out. I agreed Michael was under a lot of stress, but I didn't believe that Michael would disappear for hours without contacting me.

I got in my car and drove to Michael's office twenty minutes away. I circled the parking lot three or four times, looking for Michael's car, but the car wasn't in the parking lot. When I returned home, I texted Michael's kids and asked if they had spoken with their dad today. His son said he texted his dad earlier in the day but got no response. His daughter said she talked to her dad on the phone around 1:00 pm. She could tell he was in his car driving, and he seemed a little distracted. I tried not to alarm them, but I did say Michael should have been home hours ago, and I can't find him.

His son asked if I knew his dad's Apple ID and password so he could locate Michael's phone, but I didn't. He suggested I call BMW and ask them to find Michael's car using the GPS tracker on the vehicle. Great idea! I leased the X3 in my name. I called BMW, told them I was the car's registered owner, and asked them to locate the vehicle for me. The BMW representative informed me they required a police report to track the car. My fear and the feeling something terrible happened to Michael grew as each hour passed. I finally called my daughter and said I needed her. Dani was at my house within fifteen minutes. I called the Sheriff's department and told them my husband was missing, and I was concerned about his welfare. That was the first moment I allowed myself to consider the possibility of Michael's life in danger.

Once the sheriff arrived, my daughter, Dani, used her paralegal skills and took the lead. While I answered specific questions, the sheriff asked about Michael's birth, height, weight, and clothes. Dani took notes and communicated information back and forth between the sheriff and BMW. Once the sheriff could provide a police report number to the BMW representative, she could locate the vehicle.

The sheriff looked at me and asked, "Do you know anyone living in Palm Desert?"

"No. Why?" I asked.

The sheriff continued, "The car is in Palm Desert in a parking lot near a golf course."

Dani grabbed my laptop and entered the address the sheriff provided over eighty miles from our home. The image on Google Maps did look like a parking lot adjacent to a golf course. As Dani expanded the view on the map, she noticed the name of a hotel nearby to the same parking lot. Dani called the hotel and asked if they had a registered guest named Mike Savage, and they said yes. Dani explained the situation and requested the hotel do a welfare check on Mr. Savage. The hotel said they could not check on Mr. Savage without assistance from the Riverside County Sheriff's Department.

I live in Orange County, California, and Palm Desert is in Riverside County, California. The Orange County sheriff contacted the Riverside County Sheriff's Department and requested they send sheriffs to the hotel for a welfare check. Riverside County is over 7,208 square miles and spans from the greater Los Angeles area west to the Arizona border in the east. The Orange County sheriff could not estimate how quickly Riverside County would dispatch sheriffs to the hotel. The sheriff explained to me the report he filed was a missing person's report, and when the sheriffs made contact with my husband, they would not have the authority to make my husband contact me. Sheriffs would only be able to confirm they reached him. Before the sheriff left my house, he gave Dani the phone number to call for further questions or follow up on the request's status to the Riverside County Sheriff's Department.

Once the sheriff left, Dani asked me if she could call her brothers, Kris and Cory, to come to the house. I hesitated and asked for a few minutes to think. I was so scared. Selfishly, I didn't want to be alone if the news was terrible, but I also didn't want to see my kids' reactions if something terrible happened to Michael. But I said yes.

I don't know what time Kris and Cory arrived. I lost track of time hours earlier in the evening. Dani continued to call the sheriff's department for any updates, and eventually they confirmed two sheriff's deputies had arrived at the hotel. Still, the hotel staff would not allow the deputies to proceed with a welfare check without a supervisor from the sheriff's department on site. Therefore, the sheriffs had to wait for a supervisor to arrive on the scene. Dani finally received a call from the Orange County Sheriff's Department, confirming the Riverside County sheriffs had "made contact with Michael." With excitement and relief, Dani shared the information with the boys and me. I fell to the ground crying and thanking God. I thought the attorney was right after all; Michael needed a time-out to think. I also thought maybe Michael decided to drive to Phoenix and ask his dad for advice and was too tired to make the drive and needed a room for the night. I was so relieved that Michael was okay.

Five minutes later, an Orange County sheriff called back to apologize for relaying false information. The only information they now could confirm was Riverside County sheriffs were at the hotel in Palm Desert, and two Orange County sheriffs were en route to my house. Dani had the responsibility of telling me the information was wrong. The last thing I heard Dani say was, "Mom…the sheriffs are on their way to your house." I knew the only reason sheriffs would be returning to my home was to inform me of Michael's death. OH, GOD… NO! I CAN'T DO THIS AGAIN!

I wanted to run and hide. If the sheriffs couldn't find me, they couldn't tell me something horrible happened to Michael. I ran screaming into my walk-in pantry as my son, Cory, followed me. He put his arms around me and held me as I cried and pounded on the shelves with my fists, yelling, "NO. NO. NO." I was not going to accept bad news, not again.

When the sheriffs arrived at my house, Dani and Kris met them out-side. They tried convincing the sheriffs not to come into my house, but legally the sheriffs are required to notify the next of kin —me. When they walked into my family room, I looked at them in denial and said, "I know there's been a mistake made. I need to find my keys and drive to Palm Desert myself and find Michael." As the two sheriffs stood staring at me and shaking their heads, I could hear my kids saying, "Mom, we need you to sit down. There's no mistake."

Within the hour, the Riverside County coroner called to ask me some questions. She asked me to describe what Michael was wearing and what items he may have had with him. I told her I thought he would have his phone, iPad, laptop, and briefcase. She also asked if Michael had a his-tory of suicidal ideation. I told the coroner this was a second marriage for both of us, and I had known Michael for just over three years. I confirmed Michael was under a great deal of stress in the past week, but I didn't witness any behavior in Michael indicating he was a threat to himself. I asked the coroner if Michael left a note, and she said yes. I also asked her if Michael had anything else with him. She said, "yes, he had a box of cards." "A box of cards? Are they from me?", I asked. Again, she said, "yes." I broke down, crying, and tossed my phone to my son.

I gave Michael greeting cards for every occasion and sometimes simply because I loved him. In February, I gave Michael a Valentine's card every morning for two weeks leading up to Valentine's Day. When Michael traveled, I hid a stack of cards in his luggage, one to open each day he was away. I had no idea he was keeping all the cards.

I don't remember what happened next. Like a wounded animal, I wanted to run and hide to protect myself from more pain. Losing a husband again by suicide was unimaginable. My sense of safety and ability to trust shattered, and the gaping wound that emerged in my heart and soul was possibly not repairable. I couldn't hear or feel anything except the familiar sound of Grief's voice and her presence nearby.

CHAPTER 10

Déjà Vu

"I knew I could heal. I had done it before. I wasn't sure, however, if I had the energy and determination to do the work. Not again. Healing from the death of someone you love dearly is such hard, hard work." [1]

—Tom Zuba

NO... NO... NO...

GOD... why have you allowed this?

I CAN'T DO THIS AGAIN!

It didn't take me long to recognize Grief this time. She was all too familiar. She woke from hibernation at the exact moment I realized Michael was gone. Forever. Only Grief could hear the rapid-fire of thoughts swirling in my mind in utter disbelief. "How could this happen again? What is wrong with me? How could I be so blind and so stupid?" But this time, I welcomed Grief because Grief would be my only ally. Grief knew me, and she knew how much I loved Michael—that's the reason she was there.

BLINDSIDED

I worked hard to live again after Paul died. I kept my heart open to the possibility of loving, too. I didn't give up. I didn't wallow in self-pity and retreat. I kept moving forward even when I took steps backward. I dared to dream of a future when my heart wouldn't ache, and I would experience joy and peace again. I knew I had so much more love to give, and I believed I was worthy of being loved still. I never thought I would be widowed again by a suicide death. Never in a million years. I don't think anyone would have ever considered the possibility. Michael's death blindsided me.

Once again, I lost love. I missed the man I chose to marry, the man who brought joy and laughter back into my life, my partner, my lover, my travel companion, my plus-one, and my safe place to fall. The life I knew and cherished was gone. The same questions, the same stigma of suicide, the same complicated, messy, horrible, painful journey lay ahead. It wasn't my first rodeo. I knew what to expect, or so I thought I did. I didn't realize how I had been insulated and protected from feelings of anger over Paul's death. I could count on one hand, friends or family who shared their sense of anger toward Paul with me after his death by suicide. This time I would feel the anger. And this time, my experience would be very, very different.

Grief warned me, "Marci, everyone is going to be angry. You need to know anger is coming and be prepared."

"I hear the anger already. I see it in my kids' faces. I don't know what to do. It's my fault; I brought Michael into their lives," I thought.

If I were in my family or friend's shoes, I would be angry too! Who wouldn't be mad at what happened? I worked hard to survive Paul's death. I kept my heart open, took a risk to love again, and then without notice or explanation, I was widowed again by suicide—not because of a heart attack, or cancer, or a horrible, tragic accident. SUICIDE AGAIN! You can't make this stuff up.

In the early morning hours of March 16, my daughter asked me, "Mom, who do you want us to call?"

I said, "No one."

I needed to gather my thoughts and figure out what to do next. I was so mad at myself for calling Dani earlier in the evening, asking for her help, and allowing my sons to come over. How could I put them through this again? What was I thinking? I felt I was in the same place, not protecting my kids from pain, disappointment, or anger. I let them down and allowed their lives to be turned upside down again. Michael's death was my cross to bear, not theirs.

Grief always had an opinion on any emotion I displayed, and so she said, "This wasn't your fault. You can't deny or hide Michael's death. And you can't do it alone."

I silently screamed in my head, "I have to do it alone. I can't stand to see the pain or the anger on their faces. I can't do this again. How much is one person expected to overcome? Why can't I yell 'calf rope' and be done? I'm tapping out. I can't go through this again!"

Grief responded, "Marci, you have to go through this because you loved Michael. That's the bottom line. The days, weeks, and months ahead may seem unbearable to you right now, but you have more work to do."

Dani waited a while and then asked me again, "Mom, can I please call Diane?"

This time I said, "Okay." Within hours of receiving Dani's phone call, Diane and Dennis were on the first flight available and on their way to me – again.

ANGER AND GUILT

Because my family and friends loved me, they were angry at Michael when they learned about his death by suicide. No one could understand how Michael would die by suicide, knowing the pain I suffered after Paul's death. Eight months earlier, they attended our wedding and believed Michael's vows to me when he said, "I love you because you make me feel so proud. I love you because you believe in me even when I think I can't. I love you, Marci, because every day, you wake up smiling and laughing like it's the best day of your life. You are the dreams I never dreamed would come true. I love you because you make me say, 'Yes, we can. Yes, I want. Yes, I do.' Marci, this is the moment I've dreamt of. I don't want to forget and close my eyes and miss it. This is the moment we will remember. You are my Miracle, and I want to be yours forever."[2] They were right to believe Michael because he meant every word. Michael didn't know what the future held, and neither did I.

I wanted to run upstairs, lock myself in the bedroom for days, and cry. But I had a stepson, stepdaughter, and a second family wanting answers and information. Trying to explain the unexplainable is impossible in a phone call. Michael didn't share the stress he was under with his family. I told them about the litigation threats by two former employers, his investors' decisions to stop funding the new company, and his mounting financial debts.

Michael's parents were at their second home in Arizona when he died, and Michael's ex-wife lived in Arizona, not far from his parents. So, the family decided to gather in Arizona to wait for more information from me. Michael's son Austin, Austin's girlfriend Rebecca, and Michael's daughter Ciera flew to Arizona as quickly as possible to be with their mom. Michael's half-sister living in Seattle and one of his stepsisters residing in Northern California flew to Arizona to be with their parents. Michael's cousins living in Colorado also flew to Arizona to be with the family. No one in Michael's immediate family came to my home, so my communication with them was via phone calls in the first critical days. We didn't have the opportunity to be together in person to grieve and support each other, making the situation so much harder for me. I don't know if I ever felt so alone in my life until that day.

Michael's family expressed a range of emotions. Some families were angry at Michael and felt betrayed. Some were in shock and believed his death had to be accidental. Others harbored feelings of guilt because Michael had done this to my family and me. Because I was not with Michael's family in those first critical days, I didn't see the pain Michael's family felt. I didn't know if they thought I could have stopped him or if I should have known he was in danger.

Like five years earlier, my pain and anguish were on display. Again. Life as I had known it vanished. Again. I was overwhelmed with sadness and despair. Again. I physically ached. Again. I couldn't fully engage in conversations around me because the conversation in my mind was too distracting. Again. I begged and pleaded with God to change this outcome. Again. And still, like in a Greek tragedy, the protagonist's character and motives were judged and questioned.

After Paul died, friends and family surrounded me with love, and they did the same after hearing of Michael's death. I didn't want to put any of my family and friends through the pain again, but I don't know what I would have done without them. The unimaginable happened. The pain and suffering I fought so hard to heal from were back. The joy and love I felt in my heart were gone. My self-worth was hanging by a thread. After being knocked down again, I wasn't sure if I wanted to get up. I don't know if family and friends knew how much I needed them this time.

My cousin Diane and her husband Dennis arrived sometime on Saturday afternoon. Diane grabbed a tall glass of iced tea, a notepad, and a pen and started making a to-do list. Diane's priority was contacting the Riverside County coroner's office to determine when Michael's body could be released and contacting the local mortuary to discuss final arrangements.

Without this information, I couldn't start planning a memorial service. I wasn't privy to all the conversations behind the scenes, but I'm sure there were many.

As one of my attorneys, Dennis's priority was to communicate with my California attorneys, gather all the necessary documents needed for review, and reach out to Michael's business partners and corporate attorney regarding Michael's death. With two imminent litigation threats from two ex-employers aimed at Michael and his business partners, my attorneys acted quickly, informing all parties of the prenuptial agreement in place between Michael and myself. My daughter, Dani, is a paralegal and worked alongside Dennis, locating documents, researching records, and preparing files needed to forward to Michael's business partner and corporate attorney.

Once Riverside County completed the autopsy on Monday morning, March 18, the mortuary in Orange County dispatched their employee to pick up Michael and bring him home. I chose the same mortuary I used five years earlier for Paul. The overwhelming silence as I walked in, the smell, the endless boxes of Kleenex on every table were all too familiar. I couldn't believe I was here again. Diane was with me to hold my hand and ask the questions I couldn't: when will Michael's body arrive at the mortuary, when will his personal effects be released, when will the death certificate be available, when would cremation take place?

Tuesday morning, the mortuary called to say Michael was safely in their care, and his personal effects were available for pickup. Diane came with me to the funeral home again. This time, I waited in the car while Diane retrieved Michael's things. Once we arrived back at my house, I carried the orange bag upstairs to our bedroom, shut the door, sat down on the floor next to our bed, and cried. It took me ten or fifteen minutes to compose myself before I opened the bag. The first thing I saw was a black carry-on bag belonging to me. At first, I didn't understand why a piece of my luggage would be in the bag from the coroner's office. Then I realized

Michael stopped by our house before he drove to Palm Desert. My carry-on bag contained a large shoebox filled with various cards and love notes I had given Michael over three years. I don't know how long I sat holding the bag tightly to my chest while I cried. Each card or note is filled with my words of love, hope, encouragement, affirmation, and gratitude to Michael from me. The same cards which put a smile on his face or a joyful tear in his eye, knowing how much we loved each other, were now powerless against the deadly pain and hopelessness Michael felt on March 15, 2019.

I found his laptop, iPad, briefcase, reading glasses, Chapstick, and the DY ring he gave me two days earlier, which he planned to have resized. I also found his wallet, watch, wedding ring, the "Fighting Cancer" bracelet he wore in honor of my brother, and the bracelet he wore every day depicting the longitude and latitude of our honeymoon in the Turks and Caicos. Michael's cell phone was not in the bag, leaving me to wonder where it was. In a separate plastic evidence bag were three handwritten notes. One note was written on a hotel notepad saying, "Call my wife," followed by my name and phone number. The other two letters were personal notes, one to me and the additional message to his son and daughter.

I DON'T KNOW WHERE TO SIT

The following day I was up early and having coffee on my patio when Diane checked on me. Before Diane could say a word, I looked up at her and said, "I don't know where to sit." Instinctively, she knew what I meant. I didn't know where I was supposed to sit during the memorial service for Michael. Do I sit with my kids? Do I sit with Michael's kids, or do we sit together? What about Michael's ex-wife—where does she sit?

A few days earlier, there were discussions regarding Michael's ex-wife attending the memorial service to support their son and daughter. I knew Austin and Ciera wanted and needed their mom with them following their dad's death. I also understood their mom's need to be with them during the most challenging time in their lives. After Paul's death, my biggest priority and concern were my kids, and I would have moved mountains to be with them. But I had not met Michael's ex-wife, and the thought of meeting her for the first time at Michael's memorial service was unsettling for me. I knew I wasn't ready to make decisions I could regret. I decided it was in my best interest to postpone Michael's memorial service until further notice.

MY PAIN WAS TOO BIG FOR THE ENVIRONMENT

Even though I had been down this path before, sometimes, I underestimated my ability to navigate specific social environments. Maybe I was in denial, or perhaps I was so angry I thought I could push forward and ignore Grief again. I regret times I put family or friends in my pain and Grief path, especially the first Bunco girls' trip after Michael died. Six months earlier, the Bunco girls planned a trip to Healdsburg, California, the weekend of April 5, 2019, to celebrate the sixtieth birthday of one of our Bunco Babes. The birthday girl grew up in Healdsburg, a small town in the wine country of Sonoma County. Our Bunco group traveled together many times from New York City to Nashville to Las Vegas and many places in-between.

Healdsburg was also a place Michael and I often visited because his parents lived in Healdsburg six months out of the year. I don't know why I thought I could place myself in the eye of an emotional storm and come out unscathed. As I was packing the night before, Grief tried to warn me, but I wouldn't listen.

I heard Grief whisper, "Marci, going on this trip is not a good idea. It's only been three weeks since Michael died. You're not emotionally ready to revisit places where you have so many wonderful memories of Michael."

Stubbornly I thought, "Paul gave up on me, and Michael gave up on me! I didn't give up! I'm tired of my life changing because of their actions. Leave me alone!"

Grief was right. I wasn't ready. As much as I tried, I couldn't fully engage with my girlfriends and enjoy celebrating the milestone birthday. The conversations in my mind drowned out the conversations I wanted to hear. Wine tasting, shopping, and dining in or around the beautiful Healdsburg Plaza flooded me with Michael's memories. I didn't want to ruin the birthday festivities, but I couldn't keep the tears at bay. I wanted to go home, but I couldn't. So, I tried to distance myself from the group, which only brought more attention. In all honesty, sometimes, I struggled with life going on as usual for those around me. I'm embarrassed to admit I didn't want to hear stories of fabulous vacations or the joys of early retirement with husbands. My husbands were dead. They were gone forever. Living alone for the rest of my life was all I could imagine, and feelings of joy, contentment, and peace were beyond my reach. I couldn't articulate those feelings; all I could say was, "I don't want to do that again, or I can't do this again." I think my girlfriends heard, "I won't do this again," which caused them great concern about my overall wellbeing.

Grief is complicated and challenging to navigate. Trying to control the rapid succession of emotions is like trying to herd cats. Not *wanting* to go through the pain of losing my husband again did not mean *I wouldn't* survive the pain. My girlfriends loved me deeply and did not remain silent about their concerns for my safety. I didn't understand why they were so concerned until someone said, "Marci, we've experienced the deaths of two men we never imagined would die by suicide. We've learned a hard lesson, and we don't want to see it happen again." I finally understood their concern and realized the need to be more transparent about Grief.

CELEBRATION OF LIFE FOR MICHAEL

After returning from Healdsburg, I talked with Michael's son, Austin, and his daughter, Ciera, to get their thoughts on a Celebration of Life service for Michael. I wasn't sure when, where, or what kind of service they wanted. I told them I would understand and support a private ceremony with their mom and close relatives in Arizona or Colorado. After all, Michael and his ex-wife were married twenty-four years before their separation in January 2014, and I thought they might want to have a private family service. I also said I would travel to Arizona or Colorado for a memorial service to reduce the costs of many family members traveling to California. Austin and Ciera felt strongly any service for Michael should be held in California and include my family and friends.

Austin, Ciera, and I had an open and honest discussion about Michael's service expectations. They knew my faith was a significant part of my life and agreed to have the service in a church led by one of my pastors. We also talked about how important it was for Austin and Ciera to have their mom at the service. They acknowledged the circumstances might be difficult for their mom and me but wanted everyone to put aside personal challenges and focus on honoring their dad.

On June 15, we celebrated Michael's life in the company of family and friends at my home church, and I finally knew where to sit. I asked the church to reserve eleven chairs in the front row. I sat in the middle chair in front of the pastor with Dani, Mike, Cory, and Erin sitting to my right and Kris, Kelley, Austin, Rebecca, Ciera, and Michael's ex-wife to my left. Following the service, I hosted a luncheon at the church and dinner at my home for Michael's family, including Michael's ex-wife.

UNEXPECTED EMOTIONS OF A PRENUP

I was thankful for the prenuptial agreement Michael and I had signed before our marriage, and I was most grateful for Dennis handling Michael's business affairs on my behalf. After consulting with my California attorney, Dennis informed Michael's business attorney and his silent partner of Michael's death. Dennis also told Michael's associates of the prenuptial agreement precluding me from Michael's personal or business assets or liabilities. Dennis, Diane, and my daughter, Dani, gathered all of Michael's company-related files and sent them to his partner and attorney within the first week of Michael's passing. Michael's children, Austin and Ciera, were the only heirs to Michael's estate, and as such, they were responsible for handling Michael's affairs. I boxed up all of Michael's files, any mail he had received, and his laptop and sent them to his son. As soon as I received Michael's death certificate, I sent copies to his children. I wanted to help Austin and Ciera sort through all the daunting paperwork and help with the death notifications to Michael's creditors, bank, etc., but I couldn't. I was not legally entitled to help.

Before Michael's memorial service, I spent weeks carefully boxing up his personal belongings. I also selected several pieces of Michael's clothing and had quilts made for Austin and Ciera, just as I had done for Kris, Cory, and Dani after Paul died. The day before Michael's memorial service, I spent several hours with Austin, Rebecca, and Ciera at my house. It was the first time since Michael died where we had the opportunity to be together. I gave them the quilts and provided them the privacy to go through their dad's belongings and take what they wanted.

IT'S ALL IN A NAME—MY NAME

Call me old-fashioned, but when I married Paul in 1980, I chose to take his last name, Glidden. When I married Michael in July 2018, I decided to take his last name, Savage. I don't remember Paul and me ever discussing whether or not I would change my last name. It was a given. However, Michael and I did discuss my name change. As much as Michael liked the idea of me changing my name, he always said it was my choice. I was Marci Glidden for over thirty-eight years, and changing my name would be a lengthy process. On a very personal level, I didn't feel comfortable marrying Michael and keeping Paul's last name; I thought it would disrespect both men.

After Michael died, I called one of my insurance brokers to inform them of Michael's passing and remove him as a second driver on my auto insurance policy. After saying, "Sorry for your loss," my broker asked, "will you be changing your name back to Glidden?" I was shocked at the question. I had just shared the unimaginable news that I was widowed for the second time in less than six years by suicide, and my broker's first question was about changing my last name. Really? Why was this the first question? Was my broker suggesting my marriage to Michael wasn't long enough to count, and I could easily erase him and start over? Unfortunately, my insurance broker was not the only person to ask me if I planned to change my name back to Glidden.

SOLITARY CONFINEMENT

Dr. Jennifer Ashton, chief medical correspondent for ABC News and Good Morning America, wrote in her book, *Life After Suicide*, "So why should my kids and I have to serve a life sentence dealing with the consequences of what he did?"[3] She referred to the life after her ex-husband, Dr. Robert C. Ashton, Jr., jumped from the George Washington Bridge on February 11, 2017. I felt the same life sentence was handed to my kids and myself after Paul died. After Michael died, I thought I was in solitary confinement.

I experienced Grief in different ways after losing Michael. Living far away from Michael's family was difficult for me. On the other hand, for some of Michael's family members who found it difficult to express their Grief, the distance provided the privacy they needed. Sharing how I was feeling or my challenges was hard to communicate over the phone or through email or text, and I think some family and friends felt the same way.

No one moved in with me after Michael died. I came home from work each day to an empty and eerily quiet house—no distractions to fill my time or conversations to override the thoughts in my mind. Many times, I left my office and cried most of the fifteen-minute drive home. Grief finally had my full attention. Day after day and night after night, Grief followed me, stalked me, and whispered, "Marci, you can heal. You can find joy again. I promise." But I didn't believe Grief. I thought Grief didn't even know what to say or do this time. Platitudes and clichés were all Grief had to offer.

As the months passed, going to bed each night became more and more difficult. Rarely did I get a restful night's sleep. Many nights I woke from a dream or nightmare reaching for my husband. Surprisingly, some nights it was Michael, and other nights it was Paul. Grieving the loss of one husband is painful. Grieving the loss of two husbands is indescribable. I didn't expect to be suffering Michael and Paul at the same time.

Michael and Paul were together in only one of my dreams. Paul died eight months after buying his dream car—a 2006 Porsche 911 Carrera. I kept the car for over four years following Paul's death. I enjoyed the Porsche, but my kids enjoyed driving it more. The Porsche reminded them of their dad, and when they drove it, they felt close to him. Eventually, the Porsche needed work, and it started costing me more and more. It wasn't my dream car; I kept the vehicle more for my kids than for myself. With my kids' blessing, I sold the Porsche in January 2019.

One night, I dreamed I was standing in my kitchen making lunch. The door from the garage into the house was open so that I could see into the garage. I heard the garage door opening, so I turned to look into the garage. As the garage door opened, I could see the Porsche sitting in the driveway, and Michael and Paul were sitting together in the Porsche. I woke from the dream startled and couldn't go back to sleep that night.

I don't know what the dream represented, but it reminded me of Michael and my conversation one evening. After having dinner at one of our favorite restaurants, we were returning home, and we were in the Porsche. Michael turned the music down and said he had a question to ask me. He asked, "Someday, when we die and go to heaven, will you be with Paul or with me?" I was surprised by his question, but I felt it was the sweetest and most thoughtful question he ever asked me. I turned to Michael and said, "Well, biblically, there is no marriage in Heaven like we understand marriage here on Earth. We will be worshiping God, and there will be no more pain or sorrow. I'm sure God has a great plan for us in Heaven, and we will **all** be at peace together." Michael smiled and said, "That sounds good to me." Paul and Michael are together in Heaven now. I often think about the conversations they must be having.

Being widowed by suicide twice is unbelievably hard, devastating, and impossible to describe. I haven't found anyone who shares this experience. Yes, there are women widowed by suicide once, but not twice. If women have lost two husbands by suicide, they are not willing to be known. I don't blame them. It's a heavy burden to carry and overcome.

I struggle to find the words sufficient to articulate the emotional devastation and havoc a death by suicide leaves behind on loved ones. As a surviving spouse, I questioned my worthiness to be loved again. If and when I was ready to date, what would men think about both my husbands dying by suicide? Would they express empathy? Would they ask a few questions out of curiosity but still be willing to get to know me? Would they see me as an easy target for a quick affair and then disappear? Or would they cut and run before I could finish the sentence? All of the above!

The second time I mustered the courage and determination to trust I was worthy of love again was twice as devastating. A year and a half after Michael died, I agreed to meet a retired Air Force pilot for a Sunday afternoon walk around the harbor. He was an attractive man, with fascinating stories about his career flying an F-4. Enjoying each other's company, we stopped for a drink and a bite to eat at a restaurant in the harbor. The date was going well until he asked me how my two husbands died. I could have lied or simply said that was a conversation for another time. Instead, I laid my fork down, looked at him, and said, "They both died by suicide." With a deer in the headlight look on his face, he replied, "That puts a lot of pressure on Number three." And then silence until his cell phone rang. Quickly he answered his phone and said, "Excuse me, but I need to take this call," and stepped outside.

I signaled to the waiter and asked him to bring some "to-go" containers. When my date returned to the table, I had already boxed up our meal and asked for the check. He insisted on paying for the dinner and said, "I'm so sorry, but an emergency has come up, and I have to leave. Can I walk you to your car?" I replied, "Don't worry about me, my car isn't far away. Go take care of the emergency." I grabbed my purse and the boxed meal, said good-bye, and walked out of the restaurant to my car. As I drove home crying, Grief silently rode shotgun holding a mirror. As I glanced at my reflection in the mirror, all I could see was damaged goods.

COVID-19

As the first anniversary of Michael's death on March 15, 2020, approached, the world faced an unprecedented pandemic. A highly contagious, upper respiratory virus was quickly spreading across the globe. The World Health Organization (WHO) and the Centers for Disease Control

(CDC) issued dire warnings to global leaders and compared this pandemic to the 1918 influenza pandemic (Spanish Flu) caused by an H1N1 virus. There was no vaccine to protect against the Spanish influenza infection, and more than 670,000 Americans died. In September 1918, New York City's Board of Health required anyone with the Flu to isolate at home. Chicago leaders closed theaters, movie houses, and prohibited public gatherings. San Francisco officials recommended all residents wore masks when they were in public. Public health officials warned of the dangers of coughing and sneezing and emphasized the necessity of personal hygiene.[4]

A century later, in 2020, the United States was grossly under-prepared for a pandemic. There was no vaccine for Covid-19, testing was slow, and many individuals could carry the virus but be asymptomatic. The world was at war with an invisible killer. Healthcare systems risked being overwhelmed by not having enough medical personnel, ICU beds, respirators, and ventilators to treat Covid-19 patients. Health officials across the world emphasized the use of non-pharmaceutical measures to mitigate the spread of the virus. Non-essential businesses, schools, restaurants, movie theaters, gyms, amusement parks, sports, parks, and beaches closed. Health officials asked people to self-isolate at home, limit family gatherings to ten or fewer individuals, practice social distancing and wear masks for necessary trips to grocery stores or pharmacies. The United States economy shut down, causing economic uncertainty and high unemployment. New terms permanently branded into our daily lexicon included social distancing, contact tracing, and asymptomatic. For the first time in over five years, I didn't feel different from the rest of the world. People grieved loved ones lost to the Covid-19 virus. Others suffered from losing their job or their retirement savings. Some grieved proms and graduation ceremonies, wedding dates postponed, dining out at a favorite restaurant, attending concerts or seeing a movie, and watching sports. And most grieved the personal freedom to come and go as they pleased. The life they knew abruptly and unexpectedly changed, and uncharted waters lay ahead. Some days, it felt like the rest of the world was living the same horror movie that

I had been over the previous year— isolated, unsure, unknown territory— all a "new normal."

CHAPTER 11
Suicide Is a Game-Changer

"Nine men in ten are would-be suicides."[1]
—Benjamin Franklin

Suicide is considered one of the most challenging types of loss to sustain. Just the mention of a suicide death can change the tenor of a conversation on a dime. Death by suicide raises eyebrows and renders people speechless. It's an unnecessary traumatic ending, robbing the future and questioning the past, leaving in its wake so many unanswered questions.

Suicide is an *uncommon,* unimaginable, unthinkable, and devastating death. By 2017, it was the tenth leading cause of death overall in the United States, the second leading cause of death among individuals aged ten to thirty-four and the fourth leading cause for ages thirty-five to fifty-four, according to the Centers for Disease Control and Prevention (CDC).[2] There were 47,173 suicides, twice as many as homicides.[3] In 2017, the National Institute of Mental Health (NIMH) released staggering statistics on suicide, along with statistics on suicidal thoughts and behaviors among US adults.[4]

In the U.S., from 2001 to 2017, the total suicide rates increased by 31%. It is the only cause of death rising among the top ten leading causes.

- 9.8 million US adults had serious thoughts of suicide.

- 2.8 million US adults made suicide plans.

- 1.3 million US adults attempted suicide.

- Of the 1.3 million adults who attempted suicide, 1 million made plans before trying, but <u>300,000 made no plans before their attempt</u>.

The non-profit organization, Suicide Awareness Voices of Education (SAVE), also reports alarming suicide statistics. SAVE used the most recent data from the CDC and the World Health Organization (WHO) when compiling the following statistics[5]:

- Every day, approximately 123 Americans die by suicide—one death by suicide every 12 minutes.

- Suicide is the second leading cause of death in Americans aged 15 to 24.

- Suicide is the fourth leading cause of death in Americans aged 18 to 65.

- The highest increase in suicide is in males aged 50-plus.

- Male deaths represent 79% of all US suicides.

The risk for suicidal behavior is complex, making it difficult to predict who will act on suicidal ideations, even for the most seasoned professionals. Following Anthony Bourdain and designer Kate Spade's deaths in

2018, the New York Times published an article on how suicide has become a public health crisis. *"After decades of research, effective prevention strategies are lacking. It remains difficult, perhaps impossible, to predict who will commit suicide, and the phenomenon is complicated for researchers to study. The rise of suicide turns a dark mirror on modern American society: its racing, fractured culture; its flimsy mental health system; and the desperation of so many individual souls, hidden behind the waves of smiling social media photos and cute emoticons."*[6]

Like other illnesses, risk factors increase the likelihood someone will attempt or die by suicide. Keep in mind the following risk factors or warnings do not cause suicide.

RISK FACTORS[7]

- Mental disorders, particularly mood disorders (depression), schizophrenia, anxiety disorders, and certain personality disorders

- Alcohol and other substance use disorders

- Hopelessness

- Impulsive or aggressive tendencies

- History of trauma or abuse

- Major physical or chronic illness

- Previous suicide attempt

- Family history of suicide

- Recent job or financial loss

- The recent loss of a relationship

- Easy access to lethal means

- A sense of isolation

- The stigma associated with asking for help

- Lack of health care

- Cultural and religious beliefs

- Exposure to other people who have died by suicide

WARNING SIGNS
(INDICATES THAT SOMEONE IS IN DANGER
AND NEEDS IMMEDIATE HELP)[8]

- Talking about wanting to die or to kill oneself

- Looking for a way to kill oneself

- Talking about feeling hopeless or having no purpose

- Talking about feeling trapped or being in unbearable pain

- Talking about being a burden to others

- Increasing the use of alcohol or drugs

- Acting anxious, agitated, or reckless

- Sleeping too little or too much

- Withdrawing or feeling isolated

- Showing rage or talking about seeking revenge

- Displaying extreme mood swings

Most often, warnings do not precede suicide, and many suicides are impulsive. According to an article written in the New England Journal of Medicine in 2008, *"one-third to four-fifths of all suicide attempts, according to studies, are impulsive. Among people who made near-lethal suicide attempts, for example, 24% took less than five minutes between the decision to kill themselves and the actual attempt, and 70% took less than one hour."*[9] I will never know if Paul's or Michael's last actions were impulsive or not. But it's interesting to note until 1:00 p.m. on August 13, 2014, Paul was at work, conducting business as usual, answering emails, and returning phone calls. The coroner estimated Paul's time of death at 3:00 p.m. Only two hours between sitting in his office and sitting in a patio chair dead.

On March 15, 2019, at 10:35 a.m., I scanned the second lawsuit documents to Michael at his office. Michael emailed me back, "Thank you, sweetheart. It's going to be okay," at 10:39 a.m.

The Riverside County coroner estimated Michael's time of death between 1:00 p.m. and 2:00 p.m. Just over three hours after Michael received the scanned documents in his office in Irvine, California, Michael was dead in a hotel room in Palm Desert, California, eighty-three miles away. *"Family and friends are prone to feeling significant bewilderment about suicide. Why did this happen? How did I not see this coming? Overwhelming guilt about what they should have done more of or less of become daily, haunting thoughts. Survivors of suicide loss often feel self-blame as if somehow, they were responsible for their loved one's suicide. Many also experience anger and rage against their loved one for abandoning or rejecting them—or disappointment that somehow they were not powerful enough, loved enough, or special enough to prevent the suicide."*[10]

I never avoided uncomfortable conversations with either husband. For seven years after Paul swallowed a bottle of Lunesta, I slept with one eye open. Paul insisted it was an "out-of-body" experience and not an attempt on his life. I wasn't silent, and I remained vigilant. I asked Paul so many times how he was doing; he would get mad at me and say, "when are you ever going to forgive me? I told you I didn't try to kill myself!"

Michael's suicide blindsided me. From the time we met, I was honest and transparent about why I was a widow. Michael saw my pain and was always respectful of my love for Paul. Michael knew he was in my life because Paul wasn't. Michael never judged or disparaged the way Paul died; he would only say was, "Marci, Paul must have been in a lot of pain."

The day before Michael died, I asked, "Baby, are you feeling depressed? If you are, please tell me. I'm worried about your weight loss, and I think you need to see a doctor." Michael assured me he was not depressed. He said, "No, baby, I'm not depressed. I'm getting out of bed every day and going to work. The legal stuff is stressful, but I'm not depressed. I was depressed when I lost my CEO position in 2014... I didn't get out of bed for over a week. Don't worry, baby; I'll be okay when I get this legal stuff resolved. I'm excited about meeting with the potential investor on Monday because I think they are serious about partnering with us."

A ground-breaking Australian study from the University of New South Wales published online in January 2019 concluded that "*suicide can't be predicted by asking about suicidal thoughts.*"[11] The researchers looked at seventy major suicide studies and found two fundamental discoveries: only 1.7% of the people studied with known suicidal thoughts died by suicide. They also found that 60% of those in the study who died by suicide had denied having suicidal thoughts. Professor Michael Large noted, "*Some people will try to hide their suicidal feelings from their doctor, either out of shame or because they don't want to be stopped. We also know that suicidal feelings can fluctuate rapidly, and people may suicide very impulsively after only a short period of suicidal thoughts.*"[12] For those suffering from the loss of a loved one by suicide, Professor Large added, "*Even if they knew their relative was suicidal, the risk of death was low. And it was not their fault if they didn't know someone as suicidal.*"[13]

Like Paul and Michael, most individuals never admit or tell anyone they have thoughts about killing themselves. Not in a million years. Neither Paul nor Michael ever talked to me about feeling hopeless or wanting to harm themselves. Never. Were there days when Paul or Michael couldn't get out of bed and go to work? **No**. Did Paul or Michael talk about feeling isolated, being a burden, or showing dramatic mood swings? **No.** Did Paul or Michael talk about needing to speak with a therapist about their mental health? **No.** Was Paul or Michael stressed about business or work? **Yes.** Did Paul or Michael increase their alcohol use? **No.** Did Paul or Michael increase their use of medications? *I don't know. I will never know.*

When someone you love dies, it's soul-crushing. You're never ready to say good-bye and never prepared for the tidal wave of emotions. You long for one more conversation or one more kiss or the opportunity to tell them how very much you loved them. It's never easy under any circumstances. Rare, incurable diseases and aggressive cancers often have an unfavorable prognosis. Although family and friends may have time to prepare for the loss, no one is ever ready. Knowing how hard their loved one fought to live in the face of a devastating illness may be comforting to grieving family members.

Deaths resulting from heart failure, aneurysms, tragic car accidents, and the like are sudden and unexpected. Loved ones jolted into a new reality without warning are not ready or prepared. It's never easy. Deaths resulting from murder, or acts of terrorism, and war are devastating losses. A loved one dying while protecting the lives of others may provide comfort to grieving family and friends. Like firefighters who run back into burning buildings or soldiers sacrificing their lives for their country. But the loved ones of fallen heroes are not ready to say good-bye or prepared for the intense pain of Grief. It's never easy.

When someone you love dies by suicide, your Grief is complicated, messy, and haunting, forcing you to live with unanswered questions. Suicide is an *uncommon loss.* An unexplainable loss. A traumatic loss. An unsettling loss. A confusing and misunderstood loss. Death by suicide is contrary to the instinct to survive. Nothing about this uncommon loss makes sense, but people grieve someone they loved under all the horror and unanswered questions. Survivors of suicide deaths long for one more conversation, one more kiss, and one more chance to say *I love you.*

Suicide is a game-changer. Your loved one's life is re-evaluated, judged, and at a minimum, questioned. Curiosity replaces compassion, and anger replaces love, robbing you of the opportunity for unalloyed Grief. Exhausting and impossible questions overshadow your overwhelming pain and sadness. "What exactly happened?" "How did they kill themselves?" "Where did they kill themselves?" "Did they leave you a note?" "Are you sure it was suicide?" "Did you notice unusual behavior?" "Do you think he planned his death?" "Were there marriage or financial problems?" "Do you think they went to Heaven?" What the survivor hears is, "what did you miss?" or "couldn't you have done something to avoid this outcome?" or "didn't you see they were in trouble?" Survivors of suicide loss talk about the massive hit it takes on one's self-worth and self-esteem. Other survivors feel rejected or abandoned. The tape you replay in your head questions everything. "Did they love me?" "Why wasn't I enough?" "Did I do something that caused this?" "What could I have done to stop it?" "Why did God allow this to happen?" "Am I being punished for something?"

I get it. I've done the same thing. I've questioned why people die by suicide and have wondered what could be so hopeless that someone would "choose" to kill themselves? As if the person who killed themselves could offer a rational explanation for their exit. I remember being shocked when I learned of Robin Williams's death. I loved Robin Williams. I loved him from *Mork and Mindy*'s early days to his brilliant performances in movies like *Mrs. Doubtfire, Patch Adams, Dead Poet's Society*, and *Good Morning Vietnam*. One of my favorites was Robin Williams's Oscar-winning performance in *Good Will Hunting*. What could be so wrong in his life that he "chose" to end it all himself? I was laser-focused on "how" Robin Williams died instead of the loss of a brilliant comedian and actor. Not once did I think about his widow, his children, or close family and friends. Admittedly, I was uneducated and ill-informed on suicide, mental health issues, and deadly depression. I believed suicide was a choice. That was three days before the beginning of my very personal and intimate knowledge of suicide and its aftermath.

If Paul or Michael died from a recognizable illness or terrible accident, the general mood and tenor around me following their deaths would have been different and much easier on everyone. The big fat elephant in the room—SUICIDE—wouldn't suck the air out of the room, and no one would be walking on eggshells. But it wouldn't ever be easier for me. I wasn't thinking about how or why Paul or Michael died. The nauseating ache in the pit of my stomach and the war between denial and reality raging in my mind left me with one horrifying realization —he's gone. He's gone. Oh my God, he's gone. My heart begged for one more kiss. One more chance to say *I love you.* One more time to feel safe in his arms. One more time to hear his laughter. One more time to lie with him immersed in love so deep and intimate that the world disappears around us. Please, God, one more time to hold his hand and tell him *everything's going to be okay, baby.* Just one more time.

Paul and Michael were gone. Forever. That's what I was grieving. How Paul or Michael died wasn't my focus. I lost LOVE. I lost my future. I missed the person who knew everything about me and loved me anyway. Every cell in my body ached to see him and hold him. I thought about his last painful moments and how lonely he must have felt. The thought haunts me that I wasn't there when he needed me the most.

In the months following Paul's death in 2014 and Michael's death in 2019, I couldn't control my emotions. Sometimes I managed to hold them at bay, but not always. A song, a movie, going to a restaurant we loved, being in a town or city we visited, or something said about how they died could trigger an explosion of emotions. Their deaths shattered my heart into a zillion little pieces, and Grief lay in wait under the jagged shards. Unfiltered and off-the-cuff remarks can hurt and add more pain. If someone you know loses a spouse, child, parent, or friend by suicide, please consider the additional pain caused by the following:

Please don't say, "I understand," or "I know what you're going through," because you don't. How could you? I don't understand. Less than seventy-two hours after Paul's death, someone said to me, "I know what you're going through. I wonder if my husband might do the same thing." How could she know what I was going through? Her husband was alive and well, standing in my family room.

Platitudes and clichés are just that. Misused phrases and opinions don't require original thought and can hurt and not help. "It will get better" or "Time heals all wounds" minimizes the griever's pain. "Bad things happen to good people" and "Life isn't fair" are catchy phrases intended as words of encouragement under different circumstances.

And please don't say, "God never gives you more than you can handle." Because God does, that's the point. Why would you need God if He never allowed you to experience more than you can handle? Now is not one of those moments when you simply need to "dig down deep and pull yourself up by your bootstraps." A life ended. Many lives changed forever. Nothing is the same as it was the day before.

Please resist "fact-checking" or discounting what the griever may say. It never feels good to have your truth dismissed or questioned. The griever is in shock and may say things that don't make sense. I don't remember most of what I said in the first hours, days, weeks, and sometimes months following Paul or Michael's deaths. The intense and complicated conversations playing in my mind vacillated between denial and acceptance and every thought in-between. Widow's Brain is real.

Now is not the time to ask intrusive questions, like how did they die, did they leave you a note, do you think he planned it, or didn't you see the signs? Questions add to the stigma. It's normal to want answers, but I didn't need to feel grilled or interrogated. My whole world collapsed, and I struggled to process my new reality.

Three weeks after Paul's death, I was home when the gentlemen who serviced our pool and spa showed up for the weekly maintenance. I wanted to thank him for giving my brother a short tutorial on how the pool equipment worked. Only Paul knew how to operate the complicated pool and spa equipment. I never thought of asking Paul to teach me how to heat the spa or pool. I walked outside, said hello, and thanked the pool man for his help. He was amiable and expressed his shock and sadness when he heard about Paul's passing. He said how much he always enjoyed talking with Paul and then turned toward me and asked, "Do you think Paul's in Heaven?"

Before I turned to go back to the house, I responded, "I have no doubt Paul is in Heaven! See you next week." I made it back into my home before starting to cry. I realized the fallout from "how" Paul died would add unnecessary pain, further complicating my Grief. I spent the next hour questioning why he asked me the question? Did he think it was okay to suggest to a grieving widow that her husband may not be in Heaven, and instead is burning in hell? Or was it as simple as his lack of biblical knowledge and not meant to do more harm? Either way, it left me questioning what others were thinking. I'm not suggesting his question wasn't valid or expected it to be so hurtful. But I am saying even if it was a legitimate question and not intended to hurt, it did hurt. I doubt he would have asked the question if Paul had died any other way but by suicide.

Everyone is entitled to their own opinions and judgments on the act of suicide. That's a given and not in dispute. If you believe the act of suicide is a selfish or cowardly choice, a sin or lack of faith, or an act of weakness, understand that when you share these beliefs with a survivor of suicide, it is incredibly hurtful. A personal attack of the deceased in the company of grieving family members is harmful and inappropriate. I can't think of any circumstances when defamatory remarks about a loved one's death would be helpful and appropriate. It's akin to yelling "fire" in a crowded movie theatre; you have the right to say it, but it's not wise to do so. Judgments and opinions are just that.

I don't like to think anyone would intentionally level accusations of "selfishness" simply because they couldn't resist the temptation to criticize or offer their opinion. But whether intentional or not, it is a criticism of the deceased and shows a lack of compassion. The day after Robin Williams's death, a reporter for the Guardian wrote an article titled: "Robin Williams's death: a reminder that suicide and depression are not selfish." In the article, he writes, *"News of Robin Williams's death due to apparent suicide, said to be a result of suffering severe depression, is sad. But to say taking your own life because of such an illness is a 'selfish' act does nothing but insult the deceased, potentially cause more harm, and reveal a staggering ignorance of mental health problems."* [14]

I've had my run-ins with accusations of "selfishness" leveled at both Paul and Michael following their deaths. I attended a local fundraising event sponsored by a nationally recognized charity. I supported this charity for years, but I had reservations about attending this particular event. I knew I might see people at the event I had not seen or heard from since my husband's death. I was concerned that someone might bring up his passing and trigger my emotions. I hoped and prayed my attendance would be seen as a positive step forward, getting out of the house and socializing, and would keep the comments or questions at bay. During the event, I was standing in line at one of the numerous food stations, making small talk about how good all the food looked when someone leaned into my ear and said, "I want you to know how sorry I am, and I've been praying for you." I could have handled those thoughtful comments, but it was followed by, "It's so selfish of those men to leave you with that memory."

The comment was painful. I walked back to my table, thinking why this person would want to say something so hurtful to me and critical of Paul and Michael. I tried to enjoy the rest of the event, but all I could focus on was how different my loss is seen and thought of because it was a loss due to suicide. I left the event early when I realized those uncontrollable tears were moments away from public display. I made it out of the building but burst into tears walking through the parking lot to my car. I cried for most of the day.

For a hot minute following celebrity suicide deaths, there is usually a broad and intense discussion on the alarming increase in suicides, the risk factors associated with this type of death, the warning signs, and the available treatments. Suicide prevention phone numbers or texting numbers splash across the television with a direct plea to anyone with "suicidal thoughts" to call for help. If only it were that easy, maybe 123 people wouldn't die by suicide every day in the U.S.

Shortly after Kate Spade and Anthony Bourdain's deaths, the New York Times published an article: "How Suicide Quietly Morphed Into a Public Health Crisis." Referring to the fore mentioned celebrities, the author noted, *"They were the latest markers of an intractable public health crisis that has been unfolding in slow motion for a generation. After decades of research, effective prevention strategies are lacking. It remains difficult, perhaps impossible, to predict who will commit suicide, and the phenomenon is complicated for researchers to study. The rise in suicide rates has coincided over the past two decades with a vast increase in the number of Americans given a diagnosis of depression or anxiety and treated with medication."*[15]

The stigma attached to suicide is real! We don't ask intrusive questions or make hurtful comments when someone dies of cancer, heart disease, or Alzheimer's. We don't suggest family members missed signs of the disease or could have prevented the outcome. Why is it okay to ignore the science and research supporting mental illness as a disease and continue to contribute to a deadly stigma?

CHAPTER 12

Why?

"Sadly enough, the most painful goodbyes are the ones that are left unsaid and never explained."[1]
–Jonathan Harnish

Questions. Questions. So many questions! Sometimes I wanted to scream, "I don't know why!" but I was underwater, and they couldn't hear me. As frustrating as being asked so many questions can be, they paled in comparison to questions I asked myself over and over. *Twice? How can this be?* Widowed twice by suicide is unimaginable. I want the answers. I want explanations. I want to know what killed the instinct to survive and erased the thought of loved ones. What was so emotionally or physically painful, to replace logical thinking with hopelessness and leave both Paul and Michael with only one option.

It's normal to want to know why these deaths occurred because it's hard to live with unanswered questions. I've replayed the days leading up to both Paul and Michael's deaths, looking for the elusive "ah-ha" moment when all the pieces to the puzzle fall in place. Years spent in grief and trauma therapy and reading countless books and publications on grief recovery, suicide, depression, mental illness, and the like, searching for the answers. But it won't be good enough because the answers I'm looking for I needed long before their deaths.

Whatever **"it"** was, most likely, **"it"** was a very complex combination of biological, psychological, and environmental factors converging at once, creating a break from reality from which there was no return. My biggest fear is Paul and Michael will be remembered primarily by how they died and not how they lived. One last action erasing fifty-eight years of living. I know there will always be doubters, individuals who believe Paul and Michael chose to check out. I've witnessed reactions of shock, anger, and criticism from people after learning about their suicides, individuals who stood on the periphery of these men's lives pretending to know them. And other individuals void of compassion and not interested in what may have caused this outcome. But for those of us who loved these men, understanding and accepting the disease growing within Paul and Michael will be vital to our healing.

DEADLY DEPRESSION

My friend Christal recently returned from a European vacation. While having breakfast one morning in Prague, she read an article in the New York Times International Edition and immediately thought of me. The article "Deadly Depression" was written by Jill Halper, MD, who lost her husband to depression. Ms. Halper's medical training was in adolescent medicine, caring for adolescents with mental illness, and children with cancer. Her medical training provided insight into how differently people view these two illnesses. While acknowledging depression is not cancer, she highlights how insidious both diseases can be, and like some cancers that go into remission, so can depression. Ms. Halper goes on to say, *"Suicide is how my husband died, but depression was what killed him. His suicide was not a rational, intentional act but a complication and fatal outcome of a very complex and difficult disease. Just as cancer invades the body, depression invades the psyche. Surviving family members of patients with incurable cancer know that they were powerless to stop the progression of the disease, so are the survivors of a person with depression who dies by suicide."*[2]

Depression is a systematic illness affecting all aspects of a person's life. Dr. Angelo, John Hopkins expert and Chair of Psychiatry at Howard County Hospital, noted, *"Depression is not a mood you can just get over. It is a disease in which the brain ceases to register pleasurable activities."*[3] There are many causes of depression, like chemical reactions affecting mood and perceptions, stressful life events, genetics, medications, and medical conditions, adding to the complexity of this illness. Moreover, people with depression are likely to have other chronic diseases, such as cardiovascular disease, back problems, arthritis, and high blood pressure, to name a few.

If you have never suffered from major depression, it may be difficult to understand how a person with major depression may feel. Dr. Charles Nemeroff, chairman of the Department of Psychiatry and Behavioral Sciences at the University of Miami, explains the feeling of significant depression. *"If you think about the worst day of your life, loss of a loved one, loss of your job, the breakup of a relationship, think about feeling that way every day and not knowing why. There's a feeling of hopelessness and helplessness associated with depression that, of course, then leads to suicidal thinking."*[4]

John F. Westfall is the founding pastor of Harbor Church in the Pacific Northwest and an adjunct professor at Fuller Theological Seminary. Westfall is also the author of *Getting Past What You'll Never Get Over*, a book about dealing with life's hurts. In his book, Westfall describes his battle with depression, *"I too could be funny, perhaps even irritatingly funny. The class clown, the outrageous guy who always had a quick, funny retort for any situation—that was me. I didn't see depression and humor as mutually exclusive. In reality, they both lived quite comfortably inside me. On some level, I also believed creativity and passion were linked to the ache and angst of my feelings of depression. When depression is the air we breathe, it creates its own familiarity and connectedness with our life. Eventually, we become comfortable with its presence. We get used to feeling a certain way and no longer question whether what we are feeling is appropriate or healthy. Depression fades into the fabric of our life. It is still present; we are merely oblivious to it."*[5]

DEPRESSION STATISTICS

According to the National Institute of Mental Health:[6]

- Almost one in every five adults in the U.S. lives with mental illness each year.

- An estimated 31.1% of American adults experience a form of anxiety at some time in their lives.

- 11% of men and almost 21% of women will suffer from major depression in their lifetime.

The World Health Organization (WHO):[7]

- Recognizes that one billion people globally suffer from depression.

- Predicts that depression will be the second leading cause of disability globally, just behind cardiovascular disease, by 2020.

From the Carter Center:[8]

- A Lancet Commission reported mental disorders are on the rise in every county in the world. The commission predicts it will cost the global economy 16 trillion USD annually by 2030.

According to the American Foundation for Suicide Prevention (AFSP):[9]

- The No. 1 cause of suicide is untreated depression.

These statistics are alarming. Equally alarming is the highest suicide rate of any profession in the U.S.—doctors.[10] Researchers studied doctor suicide and presented their findings at the 2018 annual meeting of the American Psychiatric Association (APA). Their results also revealed depression affects approximately 12% of male doctors and 19.5% of female doctors. Between 15% to 30% of medical students and residents show symptoms of depression. Beth Brodsky, PhD, Associate Clinical Professor of Medical Psychology at Columbia University and the Irving Medical Center, New York, calls the high rate of doctor suicide "alarming." But she says, *"It is not surprising, given the stress doctors face. The stress starts in medical school and continues in residency with high demands, competitiveness, long hours, and lack of sleep. Stress may contribute to substance abuse, another risk factor for suicide, Brodsky says."*[11] Psychiatry ranks near the top of suicide rates compared to all other medical specialties.

SYMPTOMS OF DEPRESSION

There are several cognitive, physical, and behavioral symptoms of depression. Symptoms can include an overall depressed mood, irritability, excessive worrying, problems making decisions, fatigue, appetite changes, headaches, general aches and pains, sleep problems, angry outbursts, abusing alcohol or drugs, and heart palpitations. Becoming a workaholic and withdrawing from family or friends are also symptoms of depression. And the worst case, considering or attempting suicide.

CLASSIFICATIONS OF DEPRESSION

Major depressive disorder (MDD) or clinical depression significantly affects how a person feels, thinks, and handles daily life. Severe symptoms must be present for at least two weeks.

Postpartum depression is not the same as the "baby blues." Symptoms of the baby blues, like mild depression and anxiety, occur two weeks after giving birth. The symptoms of postpartum depression begin during pregnancy and continue after giving birth. Sadness and fear make it difficult for a new mother to care for her infant and herself.

Seasonal affective disorder occurs during the winter months when there is little sunlight and usually improves in spring and summer. Symptoms include social withdrawal, increased sleep, and weight gain.

Psychotic depression includes severe major depression and psychosis associated with delusions and hallucinations.

The fifth classification of depression is Dysthymia (dis-THI-me-a) or Persistent Depressive Disorder (PDD), a less severe but chronic form of depression lasting at least two years or more. Although individuals with PDD have some of the same symptoms as MDD, they are usually highly functional achievers capable of living as if nothing is wrong. Recognizing these individuals can be complex. A depressed mood, irritability, insomnia, low energy, fatigue, appetite changes, and feelings of hopelessness are symptoms of PDD. People with PDD are at higher risk of substance abuse and anxiety.

THE BRAIN AND DEPRESSION

The National Institute of Health spends $4.5 billion a year on brain research. Yet gaps remain in what we understand about the brain. Scientists have found a genetic code but no brain-wide neural code, and there is no complete understanding of how information is encoded and transferred from cell to cell. The advancement of several brain imaging forms helps researchers determine what biological changes in the brain can cause depression. Researchers understand which three critical areas of the brain regulate mood: 1) the amygdala, part of the limbic system, is associated with emotions like fear, anger, pleasure, sorrow, and sexual arousal; 2) the thalamus, the area which receives most sensory information and relays it to the appropriate part of the cerebral cortex, affects speech, behavioral reactions, movements, thinking, and learning; and 3) the hippocampus, part of the limbic system, plays a central role in processing long-term memory. Interestingly, researchers have found a smaller hippocampus in depressed people, leading them to believe stress suppresses nerve cell production in this area.

These three areas of the brain network together, use neurons that send and receive messages. The electrical and chemical signals, called neurotransmitters, allow communication between neurons. Researchers believe the following types of neurotransmitters play a role in depression:

- Acetylcholine - enhances memory.

- Serotonin - regulates sleep, appetite, and mood, and inhibits pain. A higher risk of suicide is linked to lower levels of serotonin byproducts.

- Norepinephrine - raises blood pressure by constricting blood vessels which may cause anxiety.

- Dopamine - plays a role in how a person perceives reality. Hallucinations and delusions are associated with problems in dopamine transmission.

Stress causes chemical reactions and responses in the body. An actual chemical response occurs in your brain when confronted with physical or emotional stress. The hypothalamus releases corticotropin-releasing hormone (CRH), which travels to the pituitary gland, causing the pituitary gland to release another hormone, ACTH. ACTH is released into the bloodstream and runs to your adrenal glands which release cortisol. Cortisol gets your body ready to "fight or flee." Studies have shown people diagnosed with depression have high levels of CRH.

DEPRESSION – A SYMPTOM OF OTHER MEDICAL CONDITIONS

Depression can be associated with other medical conditions like hyperthyroidism which can trigger manic symptoms. Hypothyroidism can lead to exhaustion and depression. Almost 50% of heart attack survivors reported "feeling blue" or have significant depression, leading to a longer recovery. Depression can also be a symptom of nutritional deficiencies like the lack of vitamin B12, immune diseases such as lupus, and degenerative neurological conditions like multiple sclerosis, Parkinson's disease, and Alzheimer's disease. Cancer and erectile dysfunction in men can also contribute to depression.

DEPRESSION, ANTIDEPRESSANTS, AND OPIOIDS

Following the deaths by suicide of Kate Spade and Anthony Bourdain in June 2018, the New York Times published an article, "How Suicide Quietly Morphed Into a Public Health Crisis." The report points out how suicide rates increased simultaneously with depression and anxiety diagnoses over the past twenty years. *"The number of people taking an open-ended prescription for an antidepressant is at a historic high. More than fifteen million Americans have been on the drugs for more than five years, a rate that has more than tripled since 2000."* [12] The article also points out, *"The aggressive marketing of opioids by Purdue Pharma and others eased some of that pain - and helped create a generation of addicts, tens of thousands of whom die each year. Opioids are the third most common drugs found in systems of suicides, after alcohol and anti-anxiety medications like Xanax, the CDC reported."* [13] In September 2019, the National Institute on Drug Abuse (NIDA) and the National Institute of Mental Health (NIMH) highlighted the link between opioid use and suicide found following studies done in 2017. One study found alarming increases in suicides involving opioids from 1999 to 2014, and the rate quadrupled in people aged fifty-five to sixty-four! Another study in 2017 found that people who misused prescription opioids had a 40-60% higher likelihood of suicidal thoughts. The opioid epidemic is deadly; 47,600 people died from overdoses related to opioids in 2017. Dr. Joshua Gordon, Director of NIMH, says, *"In the absence of a suicide note, it is difficult to assess the intentions of an individual who has died of an overdose, other than circumstantially. Concealed in the alarming number of overdose deaths is a significant number of people who have decided to take their own life."* [14]

Researchers suggest the reclassification of some overdoses. Ian Rockett, an injury epidemiologist and Professor Emeritus at West Virginia University, notes that "suicide rates have been steadily climbing, but their numbers are likely even higher." Rockett also says, *"Too often opioid-related drug overdoses aren't classified as suicides. Medical examiners usually deem these deaths as 'accidental injury deaths.' This classification doesn't consider that suicide and drug overdoses both arise from 'purposeful' behaviors."* [15] Why is the death of a professional athlete, a well-known celebrity, or a drug addict living on the streets considered an accidental overdose if they willingly ingested the drugs causing their overdose? Many obvious and newsworthy overdose deaths usually result from a deadly combination of drugs and have struggled with drug addiction. The lack of a "note" left behind automatically gives the deceased the benefit of the doubt?

DEPRESSION AND ANXIETY

According to a poll conducted by the American Psychiatric Association (APA) in 2017, approximately forty million American adults—roughly 18% of the population—have an anxiety disorder. Anxiety is the most common mental illness in the U.S. Nearly one-half of all people diagnosed with depression also have an anxiety disorder. There are numerous anxiety disorders, including separation anxiety, social anxiety, panic, agoraphobia, and generalized anxiety. When anxiety and depression are combined, anxiety produces constant worry and fear, while depression produces despair and hopelessness. Dr. Mark Pollack wrote in a press statement, "*There's a significant body of research that demonstrates that individuals suffering from anxiety disorders and depression face an increased risk for suicidal thoughts and attempts. Effective diagnosing and treating both anxiety disorders and depression, especially when they co-occur, are critical pathways to intervening and reducing suicide crises.*"[16]

PARALLEL LIVES

Shortly after Michael's death, I was talking to someone about the similarities between Paul and Michael. I remember saying something like, "I've loved two amazing and different men, but they were alike in so many ways. I didn't know how much alike they would turn out to be." Both Paul and Michael were 58 years young when they died. Both were handsome, fun, loving, caring, generous, sexy, well educated, well mannered, sometimes mischievous with a hint of a bad boy, but always played well with others. They were husbands, fathers, sons, brothers, grandpas, loyal friends, and hardworking, driven, successful businesspeople. Paul chose the path of an entrepreneur, Michael preferred the corporate world, and both invested over thirty-five years in an industry they loved and received respect from their peers and colleagues. Paul and Michael were "band geeks" in high school; Paul was a drummer, and Michael played the saxophone. Both men worked while in college and paid for their college education; Paul received a degree in Economics from UCLA, and Michael received a degree in Communications from Eastern Kentucky University. While attending college, Paul and Michael were active members of college fraternities, Beta Theta Pi (Paul) and Lambda Chi Alpha (Michael).

DEADLY SIMILARITIES

Paul and Michael shared other similarities that may have contributed to their deaths:

- Both men worked hard and were driven for financial success to provide more for their families than they had as children. Their perceived economic achievements and failures measured their self-worth and self-esteem. I think I'm safe to say that they were not alone in this line of thinking. An article in *Best Life* in June 2018, "The CEO Suicides: The Rise of Financial Post-Traumatic Stress Disorder," points to an alarming increase in deaths by suicide of some of the world's wealthiest men, successful at every point in their financial careers. Leslie Mayer, PhD, a senior fellow at Wharton School of Business and the founder of the Mayer Leadership Group, an executive coaching firm, noted, *"Financial loss can trigger feelings of self-loathing, profound shame, shattered dreams, and worthlessness. In the case of successful, highly driven businesspeople, this is magnified by the fact that the trauma ties not only to a core fear but also to a core piece of their identity. Tough and smart in business does not necessarily apply to managing one's own emotions."*[17]

- Paul and Michael suffered for years with chronic pain—Paul with degenerative arthritis back pain, and Michael with debilitating headaches.

- Paul and Michael had been diagnosed with work-related anxiety and stress.

- After years of disruptive sleep patterns, doctors diagnosed both Paul and Michael with sleep apnea.

- Both men were under the care of physicians and taking prescribed medications. The Health Insurance Portability and Accountability Act (HIPAA) protects the deceased for fifty years post-death. It prohibits me from discussing medications Paul or Michael may have had on board the day they died.

- And both men had access to lethal means: one to firearms and the other to recently filled prescriptions.

THE DEADLY STIGMA

A person doesn't wake up one day choosing to have a disease. Granted, people make risky lifestyle choices. An unhealthy diet, lack of exercise, smoking, high consumption of alcohol or drugs can lead to an array of diseases like cardiovascular disease, hypertension, Type II diabetes, high blood pressure, obesity, certain cancers, and cirrhosis of the liver, to name a few. Yet, even when a person's lifestyle may ultimately contribute to a physical illness, it is considered socially unacceptable to ridicule or blame them for their condition. So, why are diseases associated with mental health different?

Depression is not a choice, a character flaw, a mood, or a sign of weakness. Depression is often misunderstood and left untreated because of its associated social stigma or a self-perceived stigma. The stigma toward mental illness is real and prevalent, and is one reason why people who have a mental illness like depression and/or anxiety do not seek treatment. If you question the prevalence of a stigma around mental health, evaluate your initial response to learning of suicidal death. Have you ever thought of individuals who die by suicide as selfish or cowardly? Have you ever thought of an individual as weak because they couldn't handle life's challenges? Has it entered your mind that a suicidal death is an easy way out? Have you ever delegitimized an end by suicide? Before being personally affected by suicide deaths and educating myself on the causes, risk factors, and staggering statistics, I did. Eliminating prejudiced attitudes stemming from a lack of knowledge or compassion is critical in reducing suicide in our country.

Men, in particular, buy into a self-imposed stigma of mental illness. Social norms like "men don't cry" or "be tough" or "buck-up" reinforce toughness to little boys from an early age. How many times have you heard someone say, "the *only* time I ever saw my dad cry was (fill in the blank)." The stigma surrounding mental health diseases like depression can be dangerous and deadly. The shame associated with depression is far higher for men than women and a significant deterrent for men to seek help. The World Health Organization recognized a gender bias in diagnosing depression; given similar symptoms, men are much less likely to be diagnosed than women. John F. Greden, Executive Director of the University of Michigan Comprehensive Depression Center, says, "*Men have a more difficult time acknowledging, describing, or owning [mental illness] than women do. Men need to recognize that this is not something they can snap out of, and it's most certainly not a sign of weakness.*"[18]

Mental illnesses have been historically subject to stigmatization and judgment. A "stigma" in ancient Greece was a brand to mark criminals and slaves. For centuries, people suffering from depression and other mental illness disorders were tortured, imprisoned, and sometimes killed. During the Middle Ages, people who had mental illnesses were imprisoned or burned at the stake. Not until the Enlightenment period were facilities established to provide help to individuals with a mental illness specifically. American sociologist Erwin Goffman suggested, *"There is no country, society, or culture where people with mental illness have the same societal value as people without a mental illness."* [19] It's no wonder why people suffering from depression and other mental illnesses are reluctant to speak up. Instead, they often choose to suffer in silence, living a double life. Capable of exerting the physical energy to present a socially acceptable outer experience at the expense of depleting the mental strength needed to battle the illness no one sees on the inside.

AN 'AH-HA' MOMENT

The Dictionary of Obscure Sorrows, an original dictionary for emotions that do not have a descriptive term, is the brilliant creation of John Koenig. Koenig introduced new words from his dictionary to the public on a weekly YouTube web series beginning in October 2014. Koenig explained during his TEDx Berkeley talk in February 2016 the purpose behind his project. He wanted to create words to describe emotions we have felt at times but couldn't describe accurately.

The words in his dictionary give a well-deserved name to emotional feelings, usually almost impossible to describe. I came across Koenig's word, *Gnossienne* (pronounced: naw-see-enn), possibly explaining why there remain so many unanswered questions. *"Gnossienne: a moment of awareness that someone you've known for years has a private and mysterious inner life, and somewhere in the hallways of their personality is a door locked from the inside, a stairway leading to a wing of the house that you've never fully explored, an unfinished attic that will remain maddeningly unknowable to you because ultimately, neither of you has a map, or a master key, or any way of knowing exactly where you stand."*[20]

That's the best description I have seen. It helps me continue to process the "Why?" in all of this.

CHAPTER 13

Lean In

"Grief teaches you that there are two kinds of people in the world, those who are available and those who are not." [1]

–Clarisa Start

My journal entry - March 29, 2019: I need everyone to lean in. Just lean into my pain. Lean into me so I know I'm not alone. I don't expect anyone to understand. How could they? I don't know what happened, and I never will. The "why" died with Paul and Michael. I wasn't privy to those last moments. No final good-bye. No final kiss. No opportunity to say, "I love you," one more time. [2]

The death of a spouse, parent, sibling, child, grandparent, or friend is excruciating. Each relationship is unique. Pain following the loss can depend on the relationship, the longevity of the bond, and the death circumstances. Relationships are often complex, further complicating an individual's grief. And because of your personal history of loss and grief, you may question how someone else is handling their suffering, and you may feel as though you would respond differently or feel differently. But grief is not a one-size-fits-all experience.

DEATH OF A PARENT

I know adult friends who have lost one parent or both parents, becoming "adult orphans." Several of my closest friends became caretakers for their ill parents, either physically, emotionally, or financially, over weeks, months, and in some cases, years. Losing a parent at any age, suddenly or following a long-term illness, is painful. It's hard. It's sad, and it leaves a hole in your heart that no one can ever fill. You can't fix it; you have to lean in.

Although the loss of a parent is a universal experience and inevitable, young children or young adults often experience a different range of emotions from older adult children. The depth of pain and earth-shattering heartache my three children and two stepchildren continue to feel after losing their fathers is unique to them. Separately and collectively, they lost a sense of security and an irreplaceable hero. The dad that kept the Bogeyman away and made them feel safe during life's storms is gone. The dad, who cheered them on from dugouts or sidelines, challenging them always to do their best, is gone. The dad, who showed them by example how to treat, love, and respect a woman, is gone. The dad they played with, laughed with, and sought asylum from when Mom got a bit "sideways" every month is gone. The dad who worked hard every day to provide for them is gone. The dad, who offers a reassuring hug and handshake to his sons on the day they marry, is gone. The dad, who should walk his daughter down the aisle someday into the arms of her love, is gone. The grandpa to current and future grandchildren will never know is gone. I couldn't fix it; I could only lean into their pain.

DEATH OF A CHILD

I can't imagine the intense grief and longing after losing a child. My dear friends, Cathy and Dan, lost their youngest son, David, in 2001. David was the most adorable blue-eyed, red-headed little cherub I have ever had the privilege of knowing. Cathy and Dan noticed something wasn't quite right with little David's muscle control before turning one. For almost two years, Cathy and Dan searched for a diagnosis and treatment for their son, from doctor to doctor, hospital to hospital, test after grueling test, leaving no stone unturned. It wasn't until a few months before David's third birthday, doctors at a renowned research hospital in San Diego, California, offered a diagnosis, a rare mitochondrial disease of which there was not yet a cure. Their adorable, loving, always smiling son went to Heaven on July 1, 2001. The thought of their loss takes my breath away, even as I'm writing the story.

I didn't know what to say or what to do. I knew it would be hard to see Cathy and Dan and their pain, sadness, and longing for their precious son. I also knew there would be a feeling of guilt swirling in my head because my three healthy children were just a few houses away, living life as usual. All I could do was show up and pray that my presence would be good enough. I grabbed a box of Kleenex, walked down the street to their house, and walked into their pain. The only thing I remember saying was, "I don't know how you are breathing." Their suffering was unimaginable, and their pain indescribable. Their pain was and is my worst nightmare. I couldn't fix it; I could only lean in.

DEATH OF A SIBLING

A parolee murdered my friend Barb's younger brother, Coleman, in August 1991. Barb offered insight into the torturous grief felt by her family after her brother's death. "It was devastating to our family and a secret we didn't talk about except to closest friends. It was much too hard for my mom to discuss. My mom passed away six years later, and I'm sure my brother's death had a lot to do with her passing. When my brother died, I was newly married and going to the trial every day, sitting twenty feet away from the man who stabbed my brother. It was so surreal. Friends and gang members of the murderer beat three witnesses after they testified. It was all too much for my family." [3.] I can't imagine the intensity of grief after losing a loved one because of another person's evil and hideous decision.

Living with the knowledge that your loved one died, not because they were sick or in a tragic accident, but because they were targeted and murdered is unfathomable. Sometimes, there's an arrest and conviction, but not always. In this case, the jury convicted the murderer of the crime, and justice was served. But her brother was still gone. Forever. I don't understand losing a brother or sister. My siblings are all living. They are only a phone call or text away, and I can always count on and look forward to the teasing banter between siblings at any family get-together. The death of a brother or sister is painful. The murder of a sibling or any loved one is inexcusable and traumatic. You can't fix it; you have to lean in.

DEATH OF A SPOUSE

Regardless of circumstances, the death of a loved one reverberates through every fiber of your being. You can't compare losses, but not all loss changes the entirety of your life. Following my husbands' deaths, I struggled to find one aspect of my life not changed by their absence. With each husband's death, I lost my person, my other half, and my teammate. The man I gave my heart to and who knew me wholly and intimately. The man with whom I chose to do the hard work that marriage demands. The man who made me laugh and sometimes cry. The man with whom I discussed parenting strategies, negotiated family holidays, planned vacations, and dreamed of what we would enjoy in retirement—the man who made me feel safe and with whom I trusted with my life. My marriages to Paul and Michael were different in many ways, but I was all in with both husbands. And in an instant, everything changed.

- I become a single parent, aware of my mortality and my children's fear of losing their only remaining parent. I became more cautious, took fewer risks, and kept my affairs in order.

- I became responsible for all financial obligations and decisions— mortgage payments, discretionary spending, financial planning, and retirement savings, to name a few.

- I became responsible for all household chores, inside and out, from sprinkler systems and car maintenance to moving furniture and holiday decorating.

- I became the only parent available to offer advice, encouragement, and love to our children.

- The way I ate or didn't eat drastically changed. For years, dinner time was time to reconnect with my husband at the end of the day. We followed a no-television and no-cell-phone policy during dinner; this was our time. As dinner time approaches each evening, I'm not planning or cooking dinner as I had for decades. I am on the grief diet. I don't cook, and I avoid sitting at the dinner table alone. I sit on the couch while nibbling on a microwaved quesadilla, a protein bar, or popcorn if I eat dinner.

- The way I sleep changed. I went from a sound sleeper to tossing and turning most nights.

- The friends I socialized and entertained with changed. Invitations to couples' events gradually disappeared.

Every aspect of my daily routine changed, from the amount of coffee I make every morning, the programs I watch on television, where I park my car in the garage, to the eerie silence I fall asleep to every night. For the first time in my life, I know it's possible to die from a broken heart.

LEAN IN HEROES

Without permission or warning, my world changed and became unrecognizable. No one could fix it, but friends and family could lean into my pain. And they did while putting aside their pain, their sadness, and in some cases, their anger. Friends and family took care of me when I couldn't take care of myself. They were patient and accepted the fact my suffering would not end quickly. They prayed for my healing, remained hopeful, and acknowledged even the most minor steps I made forward. I call these courageous, selfless individuals my "Lean in Heroes." They didn't need to know what to do or what to say; they couldn't fix it or change the circumstances.

"The human soul doesn't want to be advised or fixed or saved. It simply wants to be witnessed—to be seen, heard, and companioned exactly as it is. When we make that kind of deep bow to the soul of a suffering person, our respect reinforces the soul's healing resources, the only resources that can help the sufferer make it through."[4]

LEANING IN HELPS

<u>**Just show up**</u>. Surrounded by people who loved me unconditionally created a safe and insulated environment. Their presence honored and acknowledged my loss. Paul's memorial service was held one week after his death and attended by hundreds of family members, friends, and business associates. I remember standing in a reception line with my three children for over two hours after the service. It was challenging, exhausting, but more importantly, healing to see such an outpouring of love and respect. Every hug, every handshake, every "I'm so sorry for your loss," translated to "we are grieving with you, and you are not alone." Powerful in so many ways.

Give a lot of hugs and then give more hugs and more hugs. Those fantastic, medicinal squeezes of love translate into "I'm here, and I got you!" They did for me. Those precious seconds of each hug made me feel loved, less isolated, accepted, and safe. Safe from a world I didn't recognize or want or chose and protected from questions, judgments, decisions, and never-ending pain. Wrapped in the arms of a meaningful hug was also a safe place to deposit those uncontrollable tears and gut-wrenching moans of disbelief and anguish.

Listen, sit, and listen some more. Dr. Alan D. Wolfeit, author and founder of the Center for Loss and Life Transition, says, *"Your friend is hurting, your role is not to change that; it's to lean into that."*[5] I continually rewound and replayed the hours and days before Paul and Michael died, looking for clues or living in the last kiss or last text or previous phone call. A friend sitting and listening to me talk or sitting with me in silence was equally helpful for me. I appreciated people who refrained from expressing their own opinions or judgments on my husband's suicide. Grieving is complicated and extremely hard to navigate under any circumstances, and is always personal. Any disparaging comments from loved ones and friends can hurt and add so much more pain even when not intended.

Be patient. In the early days after Paul and Michael's deaths, I was in emotional shock. I'm sure I said things that seemed random, disorganized, or repetitive. I did my best to make sense out of the senselessness. I was still shaking off the dust from the explosion. I remember having endless conversations, but I couldn't tell you what we discussed. I remember hoping that each time the door opened, the next person who walked in would be able to fix this. Tell me there had been some horrible mistake. Take this pain away so I could have my life back.

Appearances can be deceiving. Recently, I was on a video conference call with a group of people who had recently lost a good friend by suicide. One of the participants said, "His wife seems to be doing well. She has a lot of support; her family and friends don't let a day go by without someone checking in on her. She's a strong woman, and if anyone can survive this, she can." From the outside looking in, it may appear that way. But appearances can most certainly be deceiving. I held on to numbing feelings as long as possible to avoid the rumbling of reality closing in on me. I wanted desperately to believe what I was hearing about the strength I possessed and the ability I had to move forward. And it was so much easier to place those expectations on me and keep moving than it was to be still and surrender to reality.

The most painful moments I experienced alone— the hundreds of nights I cried myself to sleep or the days I sat for hours in silence replaying the last days and moments I had with my husband or the times I screamed, "Why didn't you take me with you?" Raw, ugly emotions remained hidden and private. The balancing act was exhausting.

Provide water and small bites to eat for the griever. Water helps flush out the excess toxins in your body, like adrenaline and cortisol, emitted when your body goes into emotional shock. I didn't feel the desire to eat or drink. It was beneficial for me when someone put a bottle of water and a small bite to eat in front of me instead of asking me if I wanted something to drink or eat. After Paul died, I remember people bringing me plates of food and reminding me I needed to eat. I imagine how frustrated they were when they returned and picked up a full plate. My friend Sheree knew I loved a particular brand of bottled water. One day she showed up with my favorite bottled water, handed it to me, and I drank every ounce with a smile on my face. After Michael died, my daughter-in-law, Erin, knew how much I loved smoothies. She started bringing me one or two smoothies a day, loaded with extra protein and nutrients. I drank them until there was nothing more in the cup for the straw to suck up.

Be proactive and specific about offering help. After Paul and Michael died, I physically and emotionally ached. The only thing I wanted was my husband alive. I couldn't find the words to describe the raw, intense emotions that continually swirled in my head and heart. I didn't have the energy or the capability to know what I needed. I couldn't ask for help. It was helpful when people just showed up, saw a need, and took care of it. I am grateful for the support I received in the early days and weeks. Continuous prayers, nourishing meals, words of encouragement, and lots of love and hugs became life-sustaining. Volunteers arranged transportation for out-of-town family and friends and helped with any memorial or funeral arrangements. Friends wrote the names of visitors, flowers received, and any act of kindness in a journal, so I knew whom to send a thank-you card. Friends ran interference on social media and monitored incoming phone calls. Friends continually attended to the basic household needs like taking the trash out, cleaning dishes, tidying up the house for the next wave of visitors. A designated "sanctuary" room in the house was made available only to me if I felt overwhelmed and needed a safe harbor. After everyone has gone home and returned to their lives, the help required down the road is different and sometimes more critical.

Please don't disappear. Dr. Jack Jordon, a clinical psychologist and co-author of *After Suicide Loss: Coping with Your Grief,* refers to our culture's basic approach to grief as the *"flu model— unpleasant, but relatively short-lived."*[6] Grief is a long-distance event, and help for the long haul is needed and appreciated. After the shock wears off and everyone has gone home, a new, unwelcome reality sets in. You are still desperately needed. Your presence provides a respite from the isolation and loneliness often felt by a grieving spouse. Actions spoke louder than words. Showing up for a brief conversation, dropping off a favorite Starbucks drink, a heartfelt card or text, an invitation to grab a bite to eat, see a movie, or go for a walk nourished my soul and provided one more step forward toward my healing.

The griever's work toward healing is hard, and this is where your work gets more challenging. I have been in your shoes many times. Your adrenaline and "jump into action" desire to help your friend or family member immediately following the death will naturally and normally wane over days and weeks and months that follow. Life goes on, and it should. Phone calls, texts, visits, etc., become fewer and less frequent. I know. I've done it. No one is at fault, and the griever is not expecting constant attention.

But the griever can continue to feel forgotten and isolated. After losing a spouse, the griever's social status has changed from being married and part of a couple to widowed and single. It can be uncomfortable and awkward to include the widow/widower in a couple's events and equally painful and embarrassing for the griever. I remember wanting an invitation to participate in social activities. It allowed me to participate or decline the request if I wasn't ready. Receiving an invitation to join in or come along was hugely important.

In my very close circle of friends, everyone I knew was married when Paul died. I didn't have any single friends. But when Michael died, my good friend, Kerstin, had recently divorced. Her marriage ending was heartbreaking. I am embarrassed to admit I was selfishly a bit happy. Now I had a single friend available to go out to dinner with, go to a movie or concert, and a willing travel partner, a friend to talk to about our new reality of being single after being married for so many years. With Paul or Michael or without Paul or Michael, I was still Marci. The Marci, who could carry on an intelligent and thought-provoking conversation, be genuinely interested in my friends' lives, who could laugh, enjoy a few cocktails or a good movie, concert, or restaurant. It meant so much to me when a couple invited me over for dinner, or to see a recently released film, or to their annual 4th of July BBQ and fireworks display or suggest I jump on a plane and come for a visit and join them for a few days on their vacation. I eagerly welcomed days, evenings, or weeks of interaction and time away from isolation. Each opportunity refreshed my desire and determination to embrace life again.

My girlfriends were good to check in with me and fill my tank with laughter, fun, and their time. Almost every day for months following Michael's death, I received a sweet card in the mail. Cards of encouragement, friendship cards, and hilarious cards. I still have them all and read them over again from time to time.

MEN CAN ALSO HELP

I believe it's harder for men to know what to do or say even when a male friend is grieving, much less a female friend. I also think a lot of men would welcome help in some tangible way if given the opportunity. I witnessed acts of service by male friends and acquaintances after Paul's death. Jay, our neighbor and a friend, noticed some light fixtures on my house's exterior weren't working. Without asking, Jay replaced all the damaged or missing lightbulbs around my house when I was at work one day. Kevin, another friend, offered to establish a website in Paul's name for family and friends to view in the year following Paul's death. The website included a video of Paul's memorial service, various photos of Paul, and a place to write condolences.

My cousin Diane's husband, Dennis, is an attorney. After Paul's death, he collected and reviewed our trust, wills, insurance policies, and suggested a step-by-step plan to tackle the daunting paperwork following Paul's death. I don't know what I would have done without help from Dennis when Michael died. There were legal limitations to what I could and couldn't do after Michael's death because it was a second marriage for both of us. Dennis notified and consulted with Michael's attorneys and business associates regarding Michael's passing on my behalf.

Months later, I came home after work one day and saw a note taped on my front door from my gardener. The letter said I had a water leak in my front yard, and I needed to call someone to fix it. Okay, I appreciated the information, but I thought, who do I contact? A plumber, my landscaper, the builder of my home? WHO? I didn't know where to start. It was easy to find where the water buildup was in my yard, but I had no idea what caused it, how to stop it, or whom to call. So, I did absolutely nothing except calmly walk back into the house, slammed the door, and screamed at Michael for not being here to handle this problem.

My journal entry - August 27, 2019: Michael, I'm so mad you aren't here. I don't know what to do about the water leak. Why aren't you here to tell me what to do? I'm so tired of being someone's widow. I hate everything about this! I chose to be your wife, not your widow. I'm so mad at you for leaving me.[7]

The following day, I knew I had to do something. I asked a neighbor across the street where he thought the leak might be coming from and whom I should call. He suggested it could be my irrigation system and to call my landscaper. So, I called my landscaper and he sent a crew out to investigate. They determined that irrigation was not the cause of the leak but noted the water leak was coming from under my driveway. Uggghhh! Eventually, I discovered I had a mainline water leak, and the original plumber would be responsible for the repair. I won't bore you with the details on how long it took to fix the water leak or the damage it caused. I realized how much I didn't know about areas of the house I had always depended on Michael to fix.

What if the sprinklers stop working, or a toilet starts overflowing, or the spa won't turn on, or the lights go out? Whom do I call? I thought how great it would be if a few male friends came over on a Saturday afternoon and gave me a quick tutorial on things I need to know around the house. I'm a good note-taker, a quick study, and would be very grateful to get a heads up on things like:

- How does the sprinkler system work, turn off, to set the timer for watering days and times, and whom to call if I need help?

- How does the landscape lighting work, how to change the times to accommodate daylight savings time, etc.?

- Where is the shut-off valve to the water, and how to turn it off and on?

- Where is the shut-off to the gas, and how to turn it off and on?

- Where are the controls to my spa, and how to shut the water off if needed?

- How often do I need to have my tankless water heater flushed out, and whom do I call to get that done?

- How do I reset the code to the garage door keypad?

- Where do I buy air filters, and how often should they be replaced?

- How do I use the BBQ grill and the Traeger smoker?

- How often should I have my heater and air conditioner serviced?

- Can they recommend a trusted handyperson I can use in the future?

- How do I add oil to my car and air to a low tire?

- How do I get the Apple TV out of my husband's name and into mine?

It was alarming to realize how many tasks around the house I was unfamiliar with because Paul or Michael handled them.

I wondered what information my husband would have needed if I had died. Would they know how to contact our house cleaner, the days she cleans our house, and how much we pay her? Would they know how to get our gardener or pool cleaner and how much we pay them each month? Would they understand what dry cleaner we use and if any clothes are ready for pick up? Would they know all the passwords to the bills I pay online? Would they know where I hide the key to the safe containing all our essential documents?

Recently, I was at a birthday celebration honoring one of my friends. Slowly, I'm learning how to attend events solo and mix and mingle and not sit at a table alone. During a conversation with some guests, I mentioned the book I was writing. I said I was currently writing a chapter with suggestions on how family and friends can help a grieving spouse. I mentioned how much I didn't know about things around the house. I relied on my husband to handle them. One of the women in the conversation said, "I secretly hope my husband dies before me because he would be lost without me. He doesn't even know the passwords to anything."

Michael's cousin, Dave, sadly lost his beautiful wife, Cathy, in December 2016. Dave is the only widower in my current circle of friends. We talk from time to time about navigating life without our spouses, the challenges we face as single parents to grieving young adults, and the complexities of grieving the loss of a husband or wife. I asked Dave what help he appreciated from female family members and friends after Cathy's passing. Dave pointed out, Cathy was ill for perhaps seven or eight years (two and a half years from diagnosis) before her death, requiring Dave to assume some of the tasks and responsibilities early on of a mom. He talked about how other moms in the neighborhood and the school welcomed him "behind the curtain into the Mom world." These moms included him in group texts keeping Dave updated on various school events, and received him into the carpool to accommodate his work schedule. Dave said, "Marci, I had to learn what size jeans my kids wore."

Shaquille O'Neal shared a funny and heartfelt story about Kobe Bryant during the tribute at the Staples Center for the legendary basketball player on February 24, 2020.

"There's no I in team," Shaq recalls telling Bryant.

"Yeah," said Bryant, "but there is an M-E in that mother[expletive]."

Before my losses, I never realized the enormous learning curve grief brings to the game. Nor did I think about all the things I would need to know if my husband died, and I was no longer part of a team, and it was only ME.

You don't have to know what to say or what to do. All you need to do is **_lean in._**

CHAPTER 14

Outside the Wake – on the Path to Healing

*"Our job is not to deny the story, but to defy the ending—
to rise strong, recognize our story, and rumble with the truth until
we get to a place where we think, Yes. This is what happened.
This is my truth. And I will choose how this story ends."* [1]
–Brené Brown, PhD, LMSW

In the summer of 1969, the last episode of Star Trek aired on NBC; Apollo 11 landed on the moon, 400,000 music lovers flocked to Bethel, New York, for Woodstock, and three West Texas siblings learned to water-ski on Lake Amistad, twenty miles northwest of Del Rio, Texas. My two brothers, Mike and Mark, and I would spend time during the summer at my grandparent's lake house (actually a double-wide trailer) in Del Rio. We spent hours swimming in the community pool, fishing on the lake, or playing outside until supper time. No cell phones, no video games, no iPads—three kids running and playing outside, relying on our imaginations to entertain us.

Learning to water ski on Lake Amistad was fun but treacherous. Cottonmouth snakes, commonly known as water moccasins, are venomous snakes living in and around the lakes in central and south Texas. Our daddy thought a deepwater start was the best way to learn waterskiing. Once we were far away from the shoreline in deep water and securely out of the pathway of other boats, Daddy would stop the boat, put it in neutral and ask, "Who's going first?" Being older, Mike and I always let Mark be the first in the water. It was not because we were overly kind to our little brother but because we made him try first to save ourselves the embarrassment. When it was your turn, you took a more tightening tug on your life vest and jumped overboard. After several long minutes wrestling with skis to get them on while treading water, you worked hard to balance yourself as you pulled your knees close to your chest while simultaneously keeping both skis straight, halfway out of the water, and pointed up. At the same time, you're trying to follow directions given from our daddy forty feet away on the boat. All the while, knowing a cottonmouth snake could slither up at any time. It turned out to be a great way to learn how to water ski. The threat of a venomous snake nearby gives you the desire to get up on the skis and out of the water as quickly as you can.

Reminiscing about learning to water ski with my brothers that summer, I smile. I close my eyes and feel the power of being pulled by the boat, the bouncing skis on turbulent water in the wake, and the freshwater spray in my eyes. Once we got the hang of getting up and staying up on the skis, it was time to attempt to cross the wake into the smoother water to the left or right side of the boat. I call it the sweet spot—where the water is calmer, with less turbulence, allowing the skis to glide across the water with less effort. That sweet spot on the other side of the wake is what I visualize when I'm doing the hard work necessary to heal following Paul and Michael's deaths. My goal is to reach calmer water ahead, where I can breathe and reset my direction for the future.

CHOOSING TO HEAL PART 1

After finding Paul's lifeless body in August 2014, I could have laid in bed, curled up in a fetal position for weeks. And no one would have expected more. After all, most, if not everyone around me, couldn't imagine what I witnessed and the trauma I experienced. I could have retreated to the memories of a life which no longer existed, replaying the past and never seeing a future. I could have added more pain to this senseless tragedy by allowing my family and friends to witness my gradual emotional, psychological, and spiritual death.

I didn't. I chose to live. I decided to take the necessary steps required to heal following a life-shattering loss. I sought therapy. I read books about grief and widows. The path to healing wasn't easy. I made mistakes. For every step I took forward, I took four or five back. I blamed myself. I questioned my worthiness to be loved. Sometimes, I pretended I was okay when I wasn't. Other times, I did what I thought would help people around me or said what I thought they wanted to hear. All the while, I kept believing I could and would be okay.

After a year and a half living with Grief, I felt I was ready to open my heart to the possibility of loving and being loved by a man again. I understood and accepted that my Grief would never go away, and I would love and miss Paul for the rest of my life. I also knew I had the desire and capacity to love and receive love again.

Fast forward to March 2019. Michael and I are newlyweds, married for only eight months, and still in the romantic and blissful season of a three-year relationship. And then, without warning, the unimaginable happens. Michael is found dead by suicide in a resort hotel room eighty-three miles from home. I am widowed again from a suicide death. And in a split second, I plunged further into the abyss—past the painful and lonely sisterhood of widows grieving the loss of a husband and past the complicated, messy, and haunting level of widows grieving one husband who died by suicide—landing in a never been seen, isolated unrecognizable place. Alone and scared, I clung to the only, never-changing anchor I knew in the storm.

MY ANCHOR IN THE STORM AND DIFFICULT DISCUSSIONS WITH HIM

Max Lucado is my favorite Christian author. In Lucado's book, *You'll Get Through This*, he suggests doing what Jeremiah did while pastoring Jerusalem through times of political upheaval, disasters, economic collapse, and death. *"Pray your pain out. Pound the table. March up and down the lawn. It's time for tenacious, honest prayers. Angry at God? Disappointed with his strategy? Ticked off at his choices? Let him know it. Let him have it!"*[2]

Through every challenge I've faced in my life, I've held on to my faith and never let go. That's not to say I have always actively and consistently walked the talk. I'm human, and I fall short multiple times every day, like everyone. There are times when I thirst for learning and study God's word. There are also times when my Bible goes unopened for months, like following Paul and Michael's deaths. Not because I didn't believe in God and His Word, but because I hadn't given myself permission to get real and express my anger at God for allowing the losses and painful aftermath.

This time was different. This time I didn't think I had the strength or desire to work at healing. Been there, done that. I took the risk to open my heart, knowing my willingness to be vulnerable could bring joy and love into my life—or more pain. And yes, I received an abundance of joy and love. I was grateful every day for a second chance to love and to be loved. I thought I could finally relax and breathe. I had weathered the storm, and the worst was behind me. I was wrong. Deadly wrong. I found myself lying on Michael's side of our bed, holding my knees to my chest in excruciating pain as I felt my heart breaking into pieces one at a time.

My journal entry: August 18, 2019 - God, I don't understand, and I am so mad at you! You could have intervened and stopped Michael. You could have stopped Paul. If Paul hadn't died, I wouldn't be in this hell again. Twice? Why? Why must I endure this pain? What did I do wrong? The ability and desire to love and be loved runs through my DNA. You know that. You allowed me to feel joy again, feel safe again, find peace again, and then You stepped aside and allowed all to be taken from me—again. For what purpose? I can't do this again. I don't want to do this AGAIN!!!

I'm afraid to be lonely for the rest of my life, but I am terrified I will eventually find comfort in my loneliness and emotionally withdraw to avoid more pain. I'm trusting You haven't abandoned me, but I CAN'T HEAR YOU OR FEEL YOU! Your silence is deafening. LET ME KNOW YOU SEE EVERY TEAR THAT FALLS. SHOW ME A GLIMPSE OF HOW YOU WILL NOT WASTE MY HURT. I can't get past my pain to read your word. The truth is I don't want words. I want to hope. I need to know I won't feel this pain FOREVER. I NEED YOU TO SHOW UP AND MEET ME IN MY PAIN.[3]

I must have fallen asleep while writing. I woke up the following day next to my journal— opened to the tear-stained page with this entry. It feels good to admit the honest conversations I had with God. I know He continues to hold me firmly in His grip, even when I can't feel Him. Here are six scriptures I placed in a Hope Box I received from my pastor's wife when I met with her following Michael's death:

"God blesses those who mourn, for they will be comforted."
(Matthew 5:4, NLT)

"Weeping may last through the night, but joy comes with the morning."
(Psalm 30:5, NLT)

"The Lord is close to the brokenhearted and rescues those whose spirits are crushed." (Psalm 34:18, NLT)

"So, God has given both his promise and his oath. These two are unchangeable because it's impossible for God to lie. Therefore, we who have fled to him for refuge can have great confidence as we hold to the hope that lies before us." (Hebrews 6:18, NLT)

"What I'm about to tell you is true. You will weep and mourn while the world is full of joy. You will be sad, but your sadness will turn to joy." (John 16:20, NIRV)

"God is striding ahead of you. He's right there with you. He won't let you down; he won't leave you! Don't be intimidated. Don't worry." (Deuteronomy 31:8, MSG)

CHOOSING TO HEAL - PART II

Healing this time would be different because healing had to be different. I needed to take control and ownership of Grief. I needed to dive deeper to explore Grief. I needed to trust Grief to learn from Grief. More importantly, I needed to remind myself that Grief's existence in my life was a direct result of loving and being loved by my two amazing husbands. I needed to admit that even with the benefit of hindsight, I would still choose the life I had with Paul and with Michael.

One evening, I ask Grief to sit with me because I had something to say. I started the conversation with, "Thank you for being my constant companion. I'm not saying I like having you here. I don't. I would give anything to have my husband as my constant companion. I prefer being a wife, not a widow. You're here because I loved deeply, passionately, and unconditionally, and I am grateful for being the recipient of their love. I have more to learn from you, and I'm ready now. I want to use what I have learned from living with Grief for the greater good. From here on out, I'm taking the lead. If I need your help, I'll ask for it." For the first time in over five years, Grief sat silent and allowed me to start taking serious steps toward healing.

STEP ONE - GETTING HELP

I sought professional help from the same therapist I saw for two years after Paul's death. When I called her and told her I was widowed again by suicide, she was shocked. She immediately moved her schedule around to accommodate weekly meetings with me. Because she helped me following Paul's death, she knew my back story; she knew my strengths and weaknesses and how I processed Grief in the past. I had a safe place to fall every week. I knew I had an advocate who had emotional, psychological, and physical health as a top priority. Her years of experience, thought-pro-voking approach, and ability to hold me accountable helped me through my darkest days.

STEP TWO - EMBRACING THE CHANGE

My great-aunt Lillian Robbins Steele turned 100 years young three months after Paul's death. She was my cousin Diane's grandmother. Lillian was born on November 21, 1914, in Texas, the sixth of eight children. She was intelligent, accomplished, independent, fearless, and a sharp dresser. As her 100th birthday approached, Lillian lived in a retirement community in Arlington, Texas. Every day she joined other residents for lunch and catch up on the community's comings and goings. Lillian always dressed to the nines, complete with pantyhose underneath her dress or slacks, match-ing shoes, coordinated jewelry, and her hair neatly coiffed. After weeks of noticing Lillian's neat and professional appearance each day, a resident asked Lillian why she went through so much trouble dressing nicely for lunch? Lillian replied, "I dress to show my respect and gratitude for the privilege of having lunch with such fine people." It wasn't long before other residents upped their game on their appearance at lunch.

Aunt Lillian was also one of the wisest women I have ever known and a great storyteller. For Lillian's 100th birthday, I flew to Texas to join the family in honoring her and celebrating her remarkable life. After the party, I had the opportunity to spend some time with Aunt Lillian before going home. As Lillian sat in her rocking chair, I sat on the floor next to her as she shared some of her best stories and life experiences. She started with the story of her birth as a three-pound preemie and how her Mama, Lulu, wrapped her in a thin blanket and tied the blanket, holding Lillian around her chest, allowing her to nurse at will. Lillian believed her Mama's decision to carry her around and allowing her to nurse continually saved little Lillian's life, followed by the story of how hers and her youngest sister accidentally caught the family home on fire when they were young teenagers. Lillian continued with other stories about growing up in a small, rural town in Texas and meeting her husband, Homer Steele.

Homer passed in 1982, leaving Lillian, a widow for the past thirty-two years. She knew Paul had died three months earlier, and I was now a widow. Aunt Lillian took the opportunity to share one more piece of wisdom with me before I left. She leaned forward from her rocking chair closer to me, took my hand in hers, and said, "Marci, you will be okay when you decide to embrace the change." I didn't understand the significance of her wise words five years ago, but I do now. *Embracing the change has been a vital step toward healing.*

STEP THREE - THE "HEALING HEARTS"
WIDOW'S RETREAT

In August 2019, I received a text from my friend Barb about an upcoming Widows' retreat in November. Barb's friend, Anne-Marie, lost her husband to a fatal brain aneurysm in 2013. Following her husband's death, Anne-Marie wrote the award-winning book, *When Their World Stops: The Essential Guide to Truly Helping Anyone in Grief.*[4] She is also the founder of the Grief and Trauma Healing Network. Anne-Marie understands the pain of Grief and dedicates her life to helping others find healing and hope from a variety of losses, including death, divorce, job loss, infertility, and more.

The first "Healing Hearts" Widow's retreat debuted in November 2019 in Temecula, California. Five widows, including myself, came together for five days in hopes of finding new paths toward recovery and healing following the loss of our husbands. Grief is heavy to carry. It sometimes feels like the weight of the world is on our shoulders from the moment we wake in the morning until we eventually fall asleep at night. Linda flew in from Florida, Bridgett drove down from Nevada, Robin traveled from Washington State, and our "international" widow, Lucy, came from Canada. My travel distance was the shortest—fifty miles from Orange County to San Bernardino County in Southern California. For the first time, I was in the company of other grieving widows.

The retreat was in a beautiful, private home perched on a hill, surrounded by vineyards in Temecula, California. There was plenty of room to assemble in common areas or retreat to our bedrooms for privacy and rest. Anne-Marie brought in a private chef who prepared delicious and healthy meals and snacks, a masseuse for massages, and an esthetician for facials. She also brought in a yoga instructor trained in techniques used for consciousness exercises. These powerful exercises taught us how to be aware of our thoughts and sensations while working through deep emotions.

Anne-Marie used a curriculum based on The Grief Recovery Handbook, written by John W. James and Russell Friedman.[5] Each morning after breakfast, we met to discuss the day's assignment. Anne-Marie thoughtfully and intentionally explained the work's purpose and goal and encouraged us to ask questions and discuss our concerns or challenges with the task. Like myself, I believe the other widows found comfort in the company of women who understood the pain of losing a husband and the challenges of creating a new life—alone. In the afternoons, Anne-Marie met with each widow separately to talk through the assignment in a private setting. The assignments were emotionally draining but profoundly healing. After dinner each night, we came together as a group to relax and unwind. We listened to music over a glass of wine, shared stories, played games, and laughed. Those last few hours of the evening reminded us we are so much more than widows; we are women who have more life to live.

I am still in awe of the depth of healing and transformation the four other widows and I experienced. We felt wrapped in a blanket of pampering love, acceptance, acknowledgment, and safety from the moment we arrived. Our time together nourished our minds, hearts, and souls, like nothing we had experienced since losing our beloved husbands. Each of us chose to heal when we decided to trust the process. And together, we came away with a renewed perspective and lifelong friendships with bunker buddies.

STEP FOUR - INVESTING IN MYSELF

I realized I was responsible only for my Grief and not for anyone else's Grief. My children's Grief, family's Grief, and friend's Grief were uniquely theirs. As much as I wanted to understand and help them through the pain, I couldn't. The best help I could provide to anyone who loved me was healing myself. In addition to professional counseling, reading countless books

MARCI GLIDDEN SAVAGE

on Grief and suicide survivors, and attending a healing widow's retreat, here's what helped me:

- I accepted the fact Grief is not linear. Grief is a complex, messy ball of yuck, able to bounce forward, backward, up and down, and around and around.

- I finally welcomed Grief as a teacher and not the enemy.

- When asked, I told the truth about my pain. I didn't say I was okay when I wasn't. The truth does "set you free."

- I actively worked to understand the cause(s) behind Paul and Michael's deaths.

- I breathed in every encouraging word and selfless act of kindness by my family and friends, reminding me I was worthy of life past Paul and Michael's deaths.

- I realized when my pain was too big for the environment. Either I avoided the potential landmines or acknowledged mistakes I made and forgave myself.

- I created a safe, comfortable sanctuary in my home, free from as many Grief triggers as possible. I chose my bedroom. I rearranged furniture, changed the bedding, and added or removed photos as needed.

- Grief is exhausting. I became aware of times I needed to relax and wait a day or two before returning phone calls or responding to texts or emails I knew could be filled with questions about how I was doing.

- I permitted myself to cry—as much as needed.

- I let go of what I believed others expected of "how I should grieve and for how long" and embraced my timetable.

180

- I made time to enjoy a lifelong hobby—genealogy research. I completed a two-and-a-half year American Genealogy: Home Study Course through the National Genealogy Society in 2013. I enjoyed researching my family history or family history for others. I spent hours each week immersed in the research I enjoyed.

- I committed to exercising a couple of times a week and gave myself grace if I didn't follow through. Over and over.

- I treated myself to a monthly, and sometimes twice a month, massage.

- I bought myself flowers two to three times a month.

- I found the courage to step out and get involved in life again.

- And I chose to move past "analysis paralysis" to tell the truth about my story, as witnessed in the previous sixty thousand-plus words in this book.

- I refused to be only a survivor of suicide loss or another statistic. Instead, I chose to be part of a solution to a growing epidemic.

I have been widowed twice over by suicide. My life today is unrecognizable from the life I had always imagined. I didn't expect two marriages to end suddenly, without warning, without a final good-bye, or be void of any chance to intervene. I can't say I didn't choose this life because I did—twice. On April 12, 1980, I wanted Paul to be my husband, for richer or poorer, in *sickness* and health until death do us part. On July 7, 2018, I chose Michael to be my husband, for richer or poorer, in *sickness* and health until death do us part. I committed to loving Paul and Michael through all things—the good, the bad, and the ugly. And I did.

Foretold is the framework of my life, but I am the architect. My heart still beats under its weathered and patina finish. I desire to live in the light of hope and possibilities, not in the darkness of Grief and the stigma of suicide. I've learned too much to stay silent. Paul and Michael's lives mattered.

Both of their legacies span fifty-eight beautiful and exciting years, not just one dark day.

As Brené Brown beautifully said, "This is what happened. This is my truth. And I will choose how this story ends." [6]

OPEN LETTER TO THE READER

I wish I could personally "thank" *every reader* who invested their time reading my story, but I can't. If I could, here's what I would say...

IF you are grieving the loss of a loved one under any circumstances, "I am so very sorry for your loss." I don't know what your Grief feels like because we have a unique and personal Grief Journey. I would also gently whisper in your ear, "There is hope, and you can heal."

IF you chose to read my story in hopes of learning how to help someone you know who is grieving the loss of a loved one by suicide, I hope you have found one or two or more ideas on how you can come alongside them in their Grief and be a *"Lean In Hero"* to them.

Suppose you chose to read my story because you had a preconceived belief about someone dying by suicide or questions about mental health issues that can lead to suicide death. In that case, I hope you have found some answers or insight about this growing epidemic.

If after reading my story, you agree, we must eliminate the stigma around suicide deaths because it's harmful and often keeps individuals from seeking the help they need - *thank you!*

Together we can eliminate the stigma around mental illness.

Together we can eliminate the stigma around deaths by suicide.

Together we can do better.

Together we can save lives.

Together we can tell Mental Illness:

Game over and Game On, insidious opponent.

We will tell.

We won't stop.

ACKNOWLEDGMENTS

Like counting the stars in the sky, it's simply impossible to personally express my gratitude to everyone who helped me navigate through the darkest and most painful losses of my life. Because of each of you, I'm still standing, still breathing, and thankfully embracing life and love. The kindness you've shown means more to me than you will ever really know.

To my children, Kris Glidden, Cory Glidden, and Dani Pratali, thank you for allowing me to reopen our shattered hearts in hopes of helping others through their pain. I love you so very much. Erin Glidden, Kelley Glidden, Mike Pratali, and Mandy Mills, thank you for your unconditional love on our good days and bad days. Austin Savage and Ciera Savage, thank you for loving and respecting me through your dad's eyes.

I'm forever grateful to my parents, LaWanda and Gene McHugh, and my family for your unwavering support and unrelenting belief that I would be okay. I love you for that. And a special note of thanks to my brother Mark and my sister-in-love Diane for always having my best interests at play and holding me firmly in prayer.

Diane and Dennis Sheehan, you're the best. Thank you for being my safe harbor through the storms. With one phone call, you put your lives on hold and raced to pick mine up from the floor. You left no stone unturned as you circled the wagons, protected me, directed traffic, did the heaving lifting, anticipated my every need, and spoke for me when I couldn't find my voice, all the while permitting me just to be. I'm eternally grateful.

A gazillion thanks to the Bunco Babes, Mii Amos, and BFFs: Sheree Timmons, Christal Cotta, Kerstin Gomez, Barb Dailey, Kathy Thomas, Rosie Garbe, Tracy Bryars, Cathy Campbell, Deborah Rice, Linda Leffel, and Donna Copenhaver. The night of August 14, 2014, you fell into my king-size bed holding me and have never let me go. With tenacity and grit, you held on when I screamed, disagreed, lashed out in anger, and cried the ugly cry. You loved me on my worst days and celebrated even the most minor step I took forward. You nourished and replenished my soul in ways I can't explain. Thank you just isn't enough.

Kathy Jo Stones, thank you so very much for your counsel, wise suggestions, and thoughtful conversations every week for years. You leaned into my pain, helped me mend my shattered heart—one piece at a time—which allowed me the will and freedom to tell my story.

I am deeply thankful for Anne-Marie Lockmeyer, Dani Cree, Renee Marcoux, and the Widows of Temecula: Bridget Stahl, Linda Maslowe, Robin Smith, and Lucy Cowal. We did the hard work, ladies. The world is our oyster. Cheers!

Dave Pfeifer, I'm so appreciative of our conversations and your willingness to share the realities and intimate details of life after losing a spouse. Your honesty, insight, and ability to articulate the emotional, psychological, and physical pain of grief were spot-on. I want to be front and center in the audience someday when you give the TED Talk the world needs to hear.

Cathy Campbell, you believed I had a story to share from the very beginning. I'm deeply thankful for the countless days you spent reading and editing the first draft at the peril of revisiting your grief. Your critique, suggestions, and nudges to dive deeper into my writing live within these pages. Now it's your turn.

Mama C (Donna Copenhaver, MSN, EdD.), thank you, thank you, thank you for editing and proofreading each citation with the skill of a seasoned wordsmith. You are the only person I know who gets excited about footnotes. And I love you for that.

To my adorable grandchildren, Colt, Kaylee, Kessler, and Carter, I love you on Monday, Tuesday, Wednesday, Thursday, Friday, Saturday, Sunday, and every second in-between.

And to MKW, cheers to family dinners on a wrap-around porch and the last best chapter. Enough said.

Special thanks to everyone on the BookBaby team who gave my story wings.

HELP IS AVAILABLE FOR YOU OR A LOVED ONE

24/7 - 365 DAYS A YEAR

National Suicide Prevention Hotline
Available 24 hours every day
1-800-273-8255

Crisis Text Line
Text **HOME** to 741741
24 hours a day, every day throughout the U.S., U.K., and Canada
https://www.crisistextline.org

Suicide Prevention Resource Center (SPRC)
http://www.sprc.org

National Institute of Mental Health (NIMH)
https://nimh.nih.gov/health/topics/suicide-prevention/index.shtml

Action Alliance for Suicide Prevention
http://actionallianceforsuicideprevention.org/resources

American Foundation for Suicide Prevention (AFSP)
https://afsp.org/find-support/resources

SAVE - founded by a mother who lost her daughter to suicide
https://save.org

The Trevor Project – a suicide prevention organization for LBGTQ youth who are especially at risk for suicide
https://www.thetrevorproject.org

REFERENCES

Forward

    1. Brené Brown, *The Gifts of Imperfection* (Center City: Hazelden Publishing, 2010), 6.

Chapter 1: Open Letter to Mental Illness

    1. "Change Direction." The White House President Barack Obama, Press Release, March 4, 2015. Obamawhitehouse. archives.gov. Accessed January 25, 2020, https:// obamawhitehouse.archives.gov/the-press-office/2015/03/04/ remarks-first-lady-change-direction-mental-health

Chapter 2: Before the Tempest

    1. Vincent van Gogh, *The Letters of Vincent van Gogh*, Ed. Ronald de Leeuw. Translator Arnold Pomerans (London: Penquin Books, 1997), 29.

Chapter 3: What Lies Beneath

    1. "Norman Cousins Quotes," Brainy Media Inc., Brainyquote.com, Accessed February 10, 2020, https://brainyquote.com/quotes/ norman_cousins_156515.

Chapter 4: August 13, 2014

    1. Nicholas Sparks, *Nights in Rodanthe* (New York: Grand Central Publishing, 2003), 152.

Chapter 5: When Everything Familiar Goes Missing

1. Lysa Terkeurst, *It's Not Supposed To Be This Way* (Nashville: Nelson Books, 2018), 72.

2. H. Norman Wright, *Experiencing Grief* (Nashville: B&H Publishing Group, 2004), 35.

3. Marci Glidden Savage, Personal Journal, September 1, 2014.

4. Rachel Naomi Remem, *Kitchen Table Wisdom* (New York: Riverhead Books, 1996), 143.

5. Marci Glidden Savage, Personal Journal, August 14, 2014.

6. Marci Glidden Savage, Personal Journal, September 10, 2014.

Chapter 6: Grief Moves In

1. Colby Baker, "Grief Sucks Said Everyone Ever," PioneerHeart. org (blog), October 2, 2015, https://pioneerheart.org/ grief-sucks-said-everyone-ever/.

2. "C. S. Lewis Quotes," Brainy Media Inc., Brainyquotes.com, Accessed November 15, 2019, https://brainyquote.com/ quotes/c_s_lewis_151481.

3. Megan Devine, *It's OK That You're Not OK* (Boulder, Colorado: Sounds True, 2017),156.

Chapter 7: Liminality

1. Sarah Addison Allen, *Lost Lake* (New York: St. Martin's Press, 2014), 136.

2. Marci Glidden Savage, Personal Journal, November 5, 2014.

3. Marci Glidden Savage, Personal Journal, January 14, 2015.

4. Max Lucado, *No Wonder They Call Him the Savior* (Portland, Oregon: Multnomah Press, 1986), 95-96.

5. Brené Brown, *Rising Strong* (New York: Random House, 2017), 4.

6. Brook Noel and Pamela D. Blair, *I Wasn't Ready to Say Good-Bye* (Naperville, Illinois: Sourcebooks, Inc.), 255.

7. Marci Glidden Savage, Personal Correspondence: letter to Paul Glidden, dated August 13, 2015.

8. Marci Glidden Savage, Personal Journal, June 3, 2015.

Chapter 8: #TakeTwo

1. John Green, *The Fault In Our Stars* (New York: Dutton Books, 2012), 260.

2. Marci Glidden Savage, Personal Journal, November 1, 2015.

3. Marci Glidden Savage, Personal Journal, December 18, 2016.

4. Tom Zuba, *Permission to Mourn: A New Way of Doing Grief* (Rockfield: Bish Press, 2014), 109-110.

5. Marci Glidden Savage, Personal Journal, March 17, 2017.

Chapter 9: March 15, 2019

1. "Hilary Stanton Zunin quote," Brainy Media Inc., Goodreads.com. Accessed February 10, 2020, https://goodreads.com/author/quotes/688159.

Chapter 10: Déjà Vu

1. Tom Zuba, *Permission to Mourn: A New Way of Doing Grief* (Rockfield: Bish Press, 2014), 3-4.

2. Michael Alan Savage, Wedding Vows, July 7, 2018.

3. Sandra Sobiera J Westfall, "ABC News' Jennifer Ashton: Life After My Husband's Suicide," *People*, May 13, 2019, 75.

4. Centers for Disease Control and Prevention. "History of 1918 Flu Pandemic." April 12, 2020, https://www.cdc.gov/flu/pandemic-resources/1918-commemoration/1918-pandemic-history.htm.

Chapter 11: Suicide is a Game Changer

1. "Benjamin Franklin Quotes," BrainyQuote.com. Accessed January 25, 2020, https://www.brainyquote.com/quotes/benjamin_franklin_133748.

2. "About Suicide and Suicide Warnings and Risk Factors." Suicide Awareness Voices of Educations. Accessed October 12, 2019, https://save.org/about-suicide/warning-signs-risk-factors-protective-factors/.

3. "Leading Causes of Death Reports, 1981-2017," Centers for Disease Control and Prevention. Accessed October 12, 2019, https://webappa.cdc.gov/sasweb/ncipc/leadcause.html

4. "Mental Health Information, Statistics – Suicide," National Institute of Mental Health. Accessed October 12, 2019, https://www.nimh.nih.gov/statistics/suicide.shtml.

5. "About Suicide and Suicide Warnings and Risk Factors." Suicide Awareness Voices of Educations. Accessed October 12, 2019, https://save.org/about-suicide/warning-signs-risk-factors-protective-factors/.

6. Benedict Carey, "How Suicide Quietly Morphed into a Public Health Crisis," *New York Times,* June 8, 2018, https://www.nytimes.com/2018/06/08/health/suicide-spade-bordain-cde.html.

7. "About Suicide and Suicide Warnings and Risk Factors." Suicide Awareness Voices of Educations. Accessed

October 12, 2019, https://save.org/about-suicide/
warning-signs-risk-factors-protective-factors/.

8. Ibid.

9. Matthew Miller and David Hemenway. "Perspective; Guns and Suicide in the United States," *The New England Journal of Medicine* (September 4, 2008), https://doi.org/10.1056/NEJMp0805923.

10. Deborah Serani, "Understanding Survivors of Suicide Loss." Psychologytoday.com (blog), November 25, 2013, https://www.psychologytoday.com/us/blog/two-takes-depression/201311/understanding-survivors-suicide-loss.

11. Catherine McHugh, Amy Corderoy, Christopher James Ryan, Ian B. Hickie, and Matthew Michael Large, "Suicide Can't Be Predicted by Asking About Suicidal Thoughts," University of New South Wales Journal 5, no. 2, (February 1, 2019), https;//doi.org/10.1192/bjo.2018.88.

12. Ibid.

13. Ibid.

14. Dean Burnett, "Robin William's Death: A Reminder That Suicide and Depression Are Not Selfish," *The Guardian*, August 12, 2014, https://www.theguardian.com/science/brain-flapping/2014/aug/12/robin-williams-suicide-and-depression-are-not-selfish.

15. Benedict Carey, "How Suicide Quietly Morphed into a Public Health Crisis," *New York Times*, June 8, 2018, https://www.nytimes.com/2018/06/08/health/suicide-spade-bordain-cde.html.

Chapter 12: Why?

1. Jonathan Harnisch, *Freak* (Corrales, Mexico: Babydude Press, 2016), 115.

2. Jill Halper, M.D., "Deadly Depression," *The New York Times International*, October 4, 2019, https://nytimes.com/2019/09/26/well/mind/suicide-depression-cancer.html.

3. "Depression: What You Need To Know As You Age," Hopkinsmedicine.org, Accessed October 10, 2019, https://www.hopkinsmedicine.org/health/conditions-and-diseases/depression-what-you-need-to-know-as-you-age.

4. David Carreon and Jessica A. Gold, "Depression: A Killing Disease," *Psychiatric Times*, April 30, 2018, https://www.psychiatrictimes.com/major-depressive-disorder/depression-killing-disease.

5. John F. Westfall, *Getting Past What You'll Never Get Over* (Grand Rapids: Revell, a division of Baker Publishing, 2012), 59-60.

6. "Mental Health Information, Topics - Depression," National Institute of Mental Health, Accessed October 12, 2019, https://www.nimh.nih.gov/health/topics/depression/index.shtml.

7. "Depression," World Health Organization. Who.int., Accessed December 4, 2019, https://who.int/news-room/fact-sheets/detail/depression.

8. "Mental Illness Will Cost the World $16 USD Trillion by 2030," *Psychiatric Times* 35,11, https://www.psychiatrictimes.com/mental-health/mental-illness-will-cost-world-16-usd-trillion-2030.

9. "About Suicide Treatment," American Foundation for Suicide Prevention, Suicide Afsp.org. Accessed December 3, 2019, https://afsp.org/about-suicide/preventing-suicide/.

10. Sara Reader, "The Physician Reluctance to Seek Mental Health Treatment," Kevinmd.com (blog), June 25, 2018, https://kevinmd.com/blog/2018/06/the-physician-reluctance-to-seek-mental-health-treatment-html/.

11. Pauline Anderson, "Physicians Experience Highest Suicide Rate of Any Profession," Medscape, May 7, 2018, https://www.medscape.com/viewarticle/896257.

12. Benedict Carey, "How Suicide Quietly Morphed into a Public Health Crisis," *New York Times*, June 8, 2018, https://www.nytimes.com/2018/06/08/health/suicide-spade-bordain-cde.html.

13. Ibid.

14. Joshua Gordon and Nora Volkow, "Suicide Deaths Are a Major Component of the Opioid Crisis That Must Be Addressed," National Institute of Mental Health, September 19, 2019, https://www.nimh.nih.gov/about/messages/2019/suicide-deaths-are-a-major-component-o.

15. Rachel Smith, "Suicide by Opioid: New Research Suggests Overdoses Should Be Classified as SelfHarm," *Kaiser Health News*, August 27, 2018, https://khn.org/news/new-research-suggests-overdoses-should-be-classified-as-self-harm/.

16. Sam P.K. Collins, "Most Americans Don't Know the True Danger of Anxiety," ThinkProgress, September 1, 2015, https://thinkprogress.org/most-americans-dont-know-the-true-danger-of-anxiety-85bc4a08dd2f/.

17. Jeff Csatati, "CEO Suicides: The Rise of Financial Post-Traumatic Stress Disorder," BestLife, June 8, 2018, https://www.bestlifeonline.com/the-ceo-suicides-the-rise-of-financial-post-traumatic-stress-disorder/.

18. Lindsay Holmes, "Introducing Shame Over: A Conversation About Men's Mental Health," *The Huffington Post*, June 9, 2018, https://twitter.com/HuffPost/status/1005562633423114243.

19. "The Stigma of Mental Disorders: A Millennia-Long History of Social Exclusion and Prejudices," European Molecular Biology Organization. EMBOpress.org. (July 28, 2016), https://doi.

org/10.15252/embr.201643041

20. John Koenig, "Gnossienne," Thedictionaryofobscuresorrows.com, Accessed October 5, 2019), https://www.dictionaryofobscuresorrows.com/ post/42192624213/gnossienne.

Chapter 13: Lean In

1. C. Start, *On Becoming A Widow* (New York: Family Library, 1973).

2. Marci Glidden Savage, Personal Journal, March 29, 2019.

3. Barb, email message to Marci Glidden Savage, January 20, 2020.

4. Palmer Parker, "The Gift of Presence, the Perils of Advice." Onbeing.org (blog). April 27, 2016, Accessed December 23, 2020, https://onbeing.org/blog/ the-gift-of-presence-the-perils-of-advice/.

5. Alan D Wolfelt, M.D., *Healing a Friend's Grieving Heart* (Fort Collins, CO: Companion Press, 2001).

6. Jack Jordan, "Suicide Survivors Face Grief, Questions, Challenges," *Harvard Health Publishing* (blog), August 12, 2014 (Updated June 8, 2018),

7. https://www.health.harvard.edu/blog/ suicide-survivors-face-grief-questions-challenges-201408127342.

8. Marci Glidden Savage, Personal Journal, August 27, 2019.

9. Nate Scott, "Shaq Drops F-Bomb in Wonderful Kobe Bryant Story at Tribute," Ftw.usatoday.com. February 24, 2020, Accessed February 26, 2020. https://ftw.usatoday.com/2020/02/ shaq-kobe-bryant-tribute/amp.

Chapter 14: Outside the Wake -On the Path to Healing

1. Brené Brown, *Rising Strong: The Reckoning. The Rumble. The Revolution* (New York: Spiegel & Grau, 2015), 50.

2. Max Lucado, *You'll Get Through This* (Nashville, TN: Thomas Nelson, 2013), 29.

3. Marci Glidden Savage, Personal Journal, August 18, 2019.

4. Anne-Marie Lockmyer, *When Their World Stops* (Anaheim, California: Joseph Allen Press, 2016).

5. John W. James and Russel Friedman, *The Grief Recovery Handbook* (New York: Harper Collins: 2009).

6. Brené Brown, *Rising Strong: The Reckoning. The Rumble. The Revolution* (New York: Spiegel & Grau, 2015), 50.